# Truth to Origin

by

Gregg K. Jann

RoseDog❧Books

PITTSBURGH, PENNSYLVANIA 15238

RoseDog Books
585 Alpha Drive
Pittsburgh, PA 15238
Visit our website at www.rosedogbookstore.com

ISBN: 978-1-4809-8002-0
eISBN: 978-1-4809-8025-9

# Contents

# Introduction

## Discovering my Tepid Past Makes Glory

Acknowledgements to Piner-Olivet Union School District; I am former elected on the Governing Board; and to the CA mental health system non-profit for us taking a chance on my benefitted person, however difficult both my struggles of negotiating their 1st union labor contract I signed for all line/ management employees and working myself off SSDI;

After my Administration standing as Chair on the Sonoma County Mental Health Board;

And to the Sonoma Democratic Party and

The Santa Rosa Democratic Club.

There are more people and places I also appreciate,

for family previously thanked not enough for my mother's "container" emotional support along with all us brothers, sisters, aunts, and uncles for a decades long time for I took for me to be a better person if I was able possible,

(I used to not be smiley pleasant, but I did self-improvement all I could; also thanks to you for the training to feel hard-nosed professional-light);

For college graduations what I needed,

And consults and lessons to The Business Degree person I am, with I wanting more remunerations.

I lived getting job early in career of Sr. Asst. Manager and Trainee, still having "wonderings" meaning.

The City I love visiting, still to be in it from Santa Rosa.

These above people, places, and traits stay.

There are people forced to be sleights who are often of the people who are getting mental health treatment for recovery, or who are the President's speech writers known to themselves or not to anyone, and people who make a difference in history in their past and going on from the present. I feel I am of these people, and we should not be ignored, kept from love no longer.

For MH consumer from author's opinion: My personal emphasis was my mind health, in spirit to realize myself. I keep a fighting attitude to improve the world I already reformed some. My role modeling overall is to get an education helping to opine intelligent thinking from me all my days of life. Also stay clean in following the law, and don't manipulate or use people. Offer good karma vibes in times for you to share if able, like your good deeds to surroundings or some words that are pleasant to talk with or lead to resolving an issue. Strategize to collaborate with the people you work with, for these might need good PR from you for available resources to you if needed. I am a counselor.

In my head-banging political writing, philosophy, and work life style; I was looking for spiritual answers, and two of the wealthiest people I met in Santa Rosa, CA said importantly from their wisdom and both personally, and meant differently than jobs or warfare. By way of trite quoting a line co-worker, "from your heart", these two top bosses said separately. 1) "apply yourself"; and then 2) "we don't want you to sacrifice yourself." I learn as quotes are shared; from reading, audiences I take part, and while doing life.

# Chapter 1

## To Do Gots

**Introductions You Can Afford**
Submitted on Wed, 2017-02-22 14:35

Introducing people can change lives. Put good faith effort in talking when they do or when it just happens in groups, as quietness may have kept you apart. The world does not bend over backward to bring us together. Accept each social opportunity like it will never again happen.

Happenstance for chances and opportunities must be persevered, for not all are noticed as caring. Our flaws must be overlooked. No smile or obese make survival of the fittest type of people banish these like psychologists rate us as human or not. The HELL with them those of ill will.

*Family and Friends*

**Using Legal Contributor by MH System**
Submitted on Sun, 2017-03-12 19:25

We who are care providers don't like it when consumers use substances for many health reasons. Both biology and socially it is toxic to live out on an addiction basis.

The Mental Health System in California USE a Tax Funder. Mr. Jann is someone providing results, insight, and de-stigma. Mr. Jann financed many local care programs throughout the state by being a source perspective designer of 2004's Prop 63 later named the Mental Health Services Act. Legislators steal credit, lobbyists lie, and Sonoma County staff and elected are bad too like the rest of them.

*Motivation*

## Cesar Chavez Day and Too Used in Poverty
Submitted on Wed, 2017-03-29 14:56

President Obama federally recognized first this Friday's holiday. Caesar Chavez combined economic justice with dignity and human rights commonly applied best making inroads in the modern era. Corruptions harm health of opponents even few legal disabled workers.

I relate by working 100-hour weeks 2 or 3 hourly jobs after designing a winning union negotiation. I bargained an unpopular stroke of history with language for consumer labor rights in a union labor contract within the mental health system. Leading up the soft white underbelly was not seen as a honest labor.

*Advocacy*

## Friends of the Land Good Peace
Submitted on Tue, 2017-04-11 20:01

Knowing those in our own land and that of other nations' animals and birds is a conversational starter point that can carry complications into habitat protections as an ethic and as hiking sports. Those Sierra Club Magazine, et. al., pictures and their legal court room battles to protect and preserve nature can, ironically perhaps to uninitiated people, feel more human in each of us; and those who are in the Middle Eastern Holy Lands too with religions touched in care. Care is humanity, and liking geology for beauty is usually kind. Extracting natural resources or developing on land needs an Environmental Impact Report, which needs to include people's preferences of beauty and nature and native heritage of long standing likeability of what made the spot or region special. It matters to care about nature, agriculture, and the local environment, acting on the wishes for the best appreciation throughout the world while protecting what we have here.

*Advocacy*

## Shared Knowledge Only in Churches Not to Withhold
Submitted on Sun, 2017-04-30 17:24

Good news came in from my late father's Protestant church where I go to bible study. Its Presbyterian, where I am the only Methodist. One went against my grain, perhaps a sermon I heard long ago. From this study I believe Jesus had a human Uncle, which I don't think I knew from my childhood. I learned from a former Catholic participant, and hopefully this is not withheld from other church bodies. Bible versions differ, and so do glorious traditions of religions and sects. Honoring the main focus of Christianity with facts that should agree, and I am a little suspect. Leaving out good role modeling or familial sense from biblical times in study can permit discrimination from others if you are not careful.

**Edit:** Then on my blog Contact Us web mail I heard John (?) was Jesus's cousin. I guess this discrimination could be why I was solitary most my adult life in this home town of mine, and I was not just a bored teenager by my quietness. I was feeling a little needy in the current group in a discrepancy about the depth of my aloneness and Jesus Easter Story while in study. As far as "main focus" and not saying the only focus is Jesus, Paul writes in letters his/some divine opinion in his first-hand experience that church members should be the same and appropriate for safety, because Paul was sometimes in jail as one Believer with who knows what. None other but the dregs of society and Jail Party controlled by Roman Centurions to this day.

The Holy Spirit theology belongs only to you, which is in all of us in Protestant Christianity. To Protestant Christian teachers one of 3 true sources of God is people who follow Christ appropriately and well, including actual Jesus the Son in prayer as the Bible teaches leaving not much for comings and goings of attitude except in playfulness as in childhood, and of course God of all creation. I was campy like clean Burlesque as a youth saying I'm God and it fits with the Royal Crowns of King Divine Right of inheritance of a minister's son to much understanding of playing among us, and in potential foreign policy for adulthood. That is this Holy Spirit is in all of us and we have a right to the Bible and its inclusiveness that God loves all and each of us. We need language like Reconciling in Methodism which we do have in Santa Rosa, CA and elsewhere in USA. For Paul in a letter says marriage and love are between a man and a woman, which yes, it's what I want, but the people among us are not all sameness and stillness.

The early church had a crowd control problem, venereal diseases ended the great philosopher era of the ancient Greeks to their memory, and forming churches needed security and The Word needed confidentiality for protection from persecution by Romans. I believe today's era is different, and we shouldn't compare US Protestant or Western World Christianity with the badness of the world that does not understand different people and punishes for difference of opinion. I try to free political prisoners with just a signature on a letter, sometimes with my peer counseling message even a plea, on Amnesty letters I get through and during church service. I know some prisoners in nations just struggle for gay rights, or are gay themselves. I may be naive in that in previous sentence, because I am not gay and never have been. It's called advocacy to fight for what's right, when it can affect people you don't know or are not like yourself and just should be treated that way.

Things like this make a person wonder of the tools he needs for future handling of his problems. I should have a Governor's Pardon, and was asked right time in a surprise to me over the phone if I wanted one. It could have been a President Pardon offered without my asking, or just a hoax. I said "No, I wanted money," to anonymous highway patrol. [My mom rolled over on her death bed in her comatose state when I loudly told her this within her stroke at her end of life.] I didn't think I needed a pardon, and that it would mean I wasn't there at The Bluff (see *Van Goghing Gregg*, 1st Chapter). I was trying in my money-making management planning and design which was the letter I sent to government health care and media people on the day to ask for the Prop 63 work I did. Maybe I should have been told I needed the pardon by family or medical staff, for I do community activist ambition and write, read elsewhere. I'm safe here with the police and my advocacy on boards and commissions, even if little recognized for great work at the state funding streams and resulting programs.

Gays have a right to serve, and we hire gay and lesbian (LGBTQ) ministers. I don't know if exclusively to Reconciling Methodist congregations. It is leading for my "Bleeding Edge of Society" like I invented the phrase of while doing computer education saying "Safety Net Economy" first and originally too. To me at least, during a dialog with Scott without coaching and no Roosevelt credits to me. I wanted the bottom levels economically better with the rising engines engaged by taxation to make kinder. I was outspoken on Aggregate Demand in Econ classes at Sonoma State helping economy more than tax cuts have a plus effect generally. It is not good for Economic degree jobs to speak so in college. I explain later more on Safety Net Economy which I started discussion in Van Goghing Gregg. It's church related by inclusive care for people even if it's government work people.

I feel like a part of victory of the throws of history in voting for a Reconciling Congregation that says "Marriage Rights;' All Means All." I'm not yet married like I want to be, for too sick previously spanning decades or too low an income wrongfully. I did not waste my time pining away suffering by not accomplishing anything as many of you looked away as we were in public board work for elections together. Thank you for bearing with me if I was too cheap for those political fundraisers, but most of you kept a place for me volunteering and I enjoy it. I wanted to learn how to run for office, and like peer counseling I learned by providing (doing). Don't just hope we will have a peace initiative titled eventually, same effort Truth to Origin on the US Constitution as an Amendment. It is just more talking points and more legal work to professionals and a harder monetization to add 2 paragraphs in 2 articles to un-Pirate Economy for MH Consumer or Victims who has more, not less, than computer internet inventor role not yet paid hopefully so.

We got first responders and National Guard in town, what do they think of such sole proprietor, independent writing meant to win peace's for this nation? Let's get this puppy work published and released on Black Friday day after Thanksgiving and let the sales fly!! Or is that what US Copy Right Office did to the Pt. Reyes mass murders and some other great legends in quickly released books for Nancy and all them First Ladies of the White House.

I am not a scoundrel pleading patriotism finally and definitely not a sleaze me. Hopefully my background did leave out unknown exploitation of me through channels of using "gaga eyed" people to those of tinsel town of Hollywood. I used to say "gaga eyed" to my people a lot when younger, before sold to spangled singer I so believe and make declarative in this non-fiction work. Its real, and it heals, and makes whole the victims of IP theft and that of criminal exploitation if results come from this more than Vanity to myself. A friendly musician or so may have spoon fed her career in a misunderstanding, and this one gaga eyed expression comes back for one former friend (I don't like such terms) said this last time I met him (he did just then explode out the door): "I'm between the P and the M. Senator Jann." Dialog famous for Presbyterian and Methodist designer, and I'm most qualified legal citizen entity able to sue for false origin anything I author.

I win history many places among people, including for election and for paid work union labor rights, and served in appointed office, after 2 college degrees in business including a stint in management. Bad comportment is my comment about personal character at too much overwork, along with Honesty and No Vices (unknown to me, not on my initiation or volition, on women's sin, lust no problem for kindness leadership – It did take explanation, and I was too fun to ask and too used and too raped to defend as Christian fed to Mental Health System godless employers), and I'm awesome in thinking- and doing- innovation with care for society in the big picture. Family is long view, and I was hurt and discriminated from having this is past, present hopefully to get my own family I want in future present tense.

**NOTE for those who have difficulty with truth and discriminated person writing or doing religion in exploring which may not end up yours.:** *My journalism says one kind of religion stole computers design from me at Chico State and beyond, I was poisoned in childhood talking priestly which belong to my rights, and I was honestly told in Bible Study a year ago we do nothing with that other religion. I guess writing here as well I am staking out territory for a new Methodism almost 2 decades old at CCUM in Santa Rosa, not on clergy order but as an author at least, on my own wild card if nothing else. I am a history-making advocate in my own right. All rights reserved for Gregg K. Jann in my advocacy and IP wants and wishes forming for me. For past IP creations I spoke, drew, planned over a lifetime, wrote, sang, reclaim, or did structured walk through or in my experience. "Larking" source perspective designs matter and mine and I were used unauthorized and stolen and both I and the Authentic Economy need to un-Pirate Western Capitalism. I have a intended public document you like enclosed. I don't want to rape my true peace meaning that we can attain through with the people-, what this is government; justice such as schools, disabled econ rights, and victims' restitution not just for one person. Pay Gregg K. Jann for credits I am, not just written pages. Read how I handle nude credits in all in 4 books I have published assuming this gets through the censors in my name, and inform me what else was stolen from me to my money, if you can.*

*I was never a bigot or racist about someone and their religion. I'm not here either. It's a crock to say a belief system makes on a member of a race in and of itself. If I live or just end of recognized by churches as a Protestant Religious Symbol, it is to bring peace, justice, and unity for freedom to more choices Protestant way. I will remain a worship service "back bencher" as I rely on my expert elders and the preachers for to guide my education, training, reflection and meaningful enjoyment to go along in with worship for Jesus. I want Peace and Prosperity to spread with a sense of better kindness and not harm.*

*Since I'm supposed to tell all my friends and family, I went to just one Self Reliance Class recently led by a man of the Church of the Latter Day Saints in my apartment building for special needs, mentally ill, or all- or partly retired. My thinking cap takes it all in, and produces my ideology and provides solace in my hard knocks as I bring it down to my heart. This class came forth on my mind for thinking back to my Parenting Ed advocacy and statements connected to my Character Ed school board goal while at POUSD. Thinking of my father a lot, surrounding those you love with church teachings on solving problems you're temporarily having with faith is useful, and I can see it would lack care if not having emotional connection somewhere in there. School can do some things better, with students for their first time ILS mainly connectional. A lack of confidentiality in such as adult budget issues is not good for Mental Health consumers. Looking for answers takes a kind word in adult education, and in this group study I read a tiny part of the Book of Mormon aloud to the group, telling this in the Truth to Origin Work for (women) so inclined. I like good, clean pussy in pretty women. Someone female needs to know such things written scatology can be overlooked and no longer denied to Gregg –...*

*Discussion started by my own dot.com blog entry about my Presbyterian Bible study, not officially or with the facilitator's approval. I don't think I am supposed to share about my theology when attributed, especially not telling people what passages I read. My privacy I want, and I gel in my thinking cap as I contemplate of messages as a gift. I am sorry about the whole thing if I am called a reporter, when it's my mind I opine.*

*I relay my joyful childhood in books. My father was respected minister of Santa Rosa 1ˢᵗ Presbyterian Church some others. He passed with a huge promotion to New York City for a church development job. IMPORTANT to my heart!! He worked throughout the USA. I loved him with opportunity to visit with him bicoastal. I remained a divorce son on no spousal support and a church body against my mother/a former church First Lady (ha!!). We were a true family.*

*I look "un-Semitic" to a Jewish person I felt safe with in my shared space from the Methodist congregation. He is false because my mother did not give birth to this disease. It's a heredity disease, and not political opinion, but used in slander. It's meant for Jewish people and their long line of breeding specifically. He said this one bad word to me the one time I ever heard it. It would scuttle my peace plan through the constitutions by hurting reputation at the politics of it. I guess I was rude about not wanting him to go to war for Israel in war gaming during one of their too often struggles. I was telling him my long-standing want of Peace surrounding Israel as simple foreign policy I wanted deeper since childhood. And Russians more human. He was talking Israel killing of lot of them, when I advocated in the parking lot coming back from a park hike I overpaid to be part. Only after he said that strangeness in a fundraiser, I looked at this word. It isn't me.*

*I remember watching a Mafia movie at the art house theater about a Jewish family and their disabled/sick son who got married to a beautiful wife with a suicide attempt in his life somewhere in the beginning. I got to thinking because this type religion's congregant is my friend who took me places with his family, and I don't see much of him since except ok downtown. I thought a while this thought not for me that he is a rich man; does he know about Microsoft and the differences between Microsoft and Seattle group of E commerce/internet people and that of Silicon Valley investors?*

*"I" am source, stolen and medicine drugged, innocent of all crime and crime was not ever charged to me. I brainstorm with creativity what is not reported to an insider like a square, honest person who studied MIS middle 1980s. I made changes in union, schools, churches, book writing, politics, and long ago was called "an issue oriented candidate" by a state assemblyman. Also for English, Psychology. The Lord is with us, in a good fight, for those reading Gregg Jann and find you do agree with author righteously and mainly.*

*I am not Reagan-light for looking into it, the Washington state basket that Reagan saw rose colored glasses over. Just stolen as a speechwriter when it was unknown to me I was one, and it could date back to Johnson era. I just am not sure, when bans happen and it shouldn't have been aimed at me. Yet I without money and you need to know my eyes are true as you read about me in my books if the experiences happened. I am a hero idealist too. I am doing justice, for economic and my finances, against conspiracy, and against maiming for difference of opinion, right here thinking on paper electronically intended for nonfiction publication.*

*We entrepreneurs all take risks. My **Teach Peace + 2** Constitution Amendment I want proposed for state ballots or US Congress to decide for the Constitutions for Gregg K. Jann's credit and his money should have its author Gregg K. Jann come clean. I want all advocacy I do included not just school board work I advocate and authored and now in naming it with the work associated: **Truth to Origin** Amendment, read on and it's in Chapter 5. I may be promoted to religious author from only philosophy, and my politics mainstay is in the bag with economics. This one of my personal note and explanation done.*

Catholics are taught "you" in secular school as third person single and plural to understand and accept other people and types who may be a different religion than Vatican themes and Rome's mind/body controls that I was punished with. I'm hoping for non-discrimination for The Advocates many kinds as activity worth US Constitution (see later) and one is this author who wanted to get married to a beautiful female wife as soon as possible knowing it would be a long time wait when money and health is to him a while ago. It is care never to be forced in a lock up as an inmate in a hospital or jail, on just the expenses of your life and of course the harm done to you, self and to the innocent victims all. It would hurt a nice guy, who is me, to be in there. What is the big idea for not honoring me with complete recovery mind, body, and property- not in any list order?

The advocate denied some people of USA a hero by Gregg K. Jann himself being the best or only one of a unique success kindness there is in that not demagogic, Demographic form – like he may have filtered to Jesuit Jewish jailer playing sports as a youth together that Israel may want to deny a hero to its enemies. – A "Rivulet" said from me 2$^{nd}$ view to let enemy have their heroes if agreeable to our interests enough like a treaty holder.

I was just a kid when I said that changing, and I think we repeat naturally from within, not knowing where or even if what I wisely say is sold to leadership anywhere. War type things could be taken without permission like I say I was stolen very much. I bet I told a Chico State grad who was my buddy while I was struggling through course work passing and graduating. I told stuff and/or heard both or all computer, war gaming, and my computer printout of "Left" also for Conscientious Objector status only if needed my way as I was going to use it for computer design for "I-net", my wording. I believe to that D. O. D. employee or just him as successful applicant I was scary with. I think we won, me with more recovery my peers in college didn't hear from me needing and some Cold War melting from my writing as inspiration. Money and awards true, when?

I know your name college buddy, as you may remember me calling you and asking for help with movies recovery. I was slouchy sometimes with Ed, when hanging out with the gang of us. Mike the red-haired man married a Chinese. No one told me Catholics don't know you after youth like it appears I drifted apart. I was told they don't remarry due to not believing in freedom to divorce with just cause. Children have to know this just written past sentence. I met the hazy verbal agreement I had with somebody regarding Mr. Ronald Reagan in *Van Goghing Gregg* by Gregg K. Jann. Let's make a better country with a treaty for my money.

Getting back to where we were in youth. A "Rivulet" is brain function biology mass trying to and with the effects of changing attitude worth loving outlook, relations, and not just view point that makes a healthy brain build more crevassing from use. It makes for a wise form of happiness at old age as we grow intellect and feeling. I think I stated this "Rivulet" word first and originally as a nude credit with bearing, with my professional dad and friendly neighbors as too young a youth under them my wing or stealing me or holding to me better first later taught at Sonoma State to me. Or maybe I just heard it from bright people from my dialog and I will stand corrected in this one word because I didn't do my research not even looking up this "Rivulet" term in the library for etymology.

I think it flows from a small, even tiny creek sand bank or bar with water flowing and making crevasses, as the brook continued this sand bar looked like a surface cut out of a brain. I think this whole term started or I first applied it to a place in between on the way to where we spread my mother's ashes, for A Jann Hill for Mom Alice years later after this childhood instance.

I do no Criminal Trespassing with a trademark professionally filed for work in a field that has it and with like no copy right violations. I do make up words without my own false origin and copy right creative writing nonfiction format what is in re-memory from myself in my experience proven true or taught later in school I remember after I may have stated the phrase first. It is just that words, simple stuff, and no honesty in crediting sources are important to religions of the world except Christianity for the most part, and not at all to Capitalism. Don't ask a lawyer to help here, as it is the wrong profession not to threaten a lawsuit when religion wants to get something done.

I was told in MINS class at Chico State by a PhD professor from statistics still there, "Don't use a lawyer." Was he giving our college's educated people and my own work planning and design to the Roman Catholics that he may be part of, or just to the Gates team? Jerry Brown governs mostly with the Jesuit sect of Roman Catholics, and he's is in office presently at US copyright time of this "Epic Tomes IV" book application of **Truth to Origin** *by Elected Survivor.* I am not un-Semitic, we presumed journalists have to come up with something) one, and two), I work with a new form of Methodist Church. Church structures of beliefs and ideology practices and some teachings, although based on the same Bible (I don't know if this is true or not), must be different as clear as a chiming bell to a different bell of another chord. Church denominations are not named the same, so the way the thinking goes on can be agreeable to a wide stripe of Protestant Christianity but Catholics get threatened with their Market Share glory with their looting and plunder that we know for sure. It is present day, not just their whole history of punishing science and people.

Do you know if Catholic men and their wives kept my internet company from developing peace themes and growing? I was hurt by these guys as we can read in this work of *Truth to Origin* by *Elected Survivor* in my "sex blindness", I believe I my 2nd passport states wrongfully I was a chemical subject hurt to be dependent unable to create money making endeavor (a legalism for reader); third the hurt on me by Gates or his wife and team is to my income if the money trust does not print up money, transfers of cash, grants, and awards to me, (Gregg K. Jann) .

When we were young, I think the kids playing softball figurative around me always knew and wanted me in the mix of world history, and I didn't even take for granted or know for sure if I would find a female wife because she had to be beautiful. I don't want a male one. I was completely ignored by women, except I can say I never smoked a tobacco cigarette and said "no" to 2 young women to smoking, both these two were on my Facebook.com last time I checked. I puffed a cigarette 3 times one New Year's Eve with Scott my brother, and some friends in Third Grade '71 for my entire history of smoking. Somebody led me falsely and said in the newspaper described me generally with smoker's teeth for formerly having tetracycline stain still showing on pictures when my teeth are white like an angel.

*Holistic Community and Permaculture*

## Taking Demotions in Career Adjustments

Submitted on Mon, 2017-05-15 15:35

Struggling with health conditions that border on disability basically require settling on lower expectations in the job market place. This is when performance is reduced, or when the symptoms are known showing or by reputation, or you use a Case Manager or some other helper. (**Tangent** where I'm from, may not be taught by all in disability movement and I see what I did not say kept me lonely too. At least I may not have or did not win friends to keep. Hide your disability to get and keep the job and its more than rude to reveal others at work who break what should be confidential for lacking fortitude. It is personal information and not the work place's business. If you did not break the law, you should not have a case manager.

"It looks weak to me," is them Managers responding group US Industrial Psychology agreement think if you feel like disclosing to someone voluntarily as they carry stigma at any position a MH consumer has in working. These business managers are concerned about losing property rights of their business to case management. CMs go behind the consumers back in their usual role, and may tell you they contribute nothing. I want Job Developers and Vocational Coaches umbrella to have no ownership rights of their clients within the Jann Amendment.

A consumer telling a co-worker gets to the manager and interference or trouble as much as sabotage to your mental status to firing happen. Tell HR and your supervisor your benefit deal to work within constraints of finances and work length of hours/schedule, without disclosing illness/disability level if you don't have to as your best strength. If you want to be self-made or last awhile like I have done in past for a good 10 years making waves and creating history that guided the channeling for future others.

**Continued.** I was known as an at-risk of re-aggravating my disability as a workaholic only at non-profit CSN for all I was involved doing to share my personal experience wanted well by work in a peer counseling role but not for my position title for confidentiality. Here I developed "clergymen blindness" as far as prevalent to me for trying IT not known certainly to me with sexy 20 years something women with my "childhood priest abuse" which deteriorated me. I struggled not knowing the cure of this in how to get married in time for babies as I race the clock to 58 years old like my personal life emulated in an unrelated to me letter Dad deadline is what I meant. I never knew it if I ever experienced sex up to copy right send-in date, and currently at copy right leave something to explain to a nice wife as if she were ever to be.

I think I told my unknown each of my sex partners I didn't see them as the activity we were doing was not the routine and a turn on perhaps, and maybe I never knew where my cock was going or knew at the time and completely forgot the memory of it till unclear, hazy later never sure of the incident maybe several. I mentioned this "sex blindness" done by clergy allegedly, or by medicine if illegal person without a courtroom trial proven by The Bluff. Used unsure to control me without a trial to my father last time I saw him in his recliner chair in Fountain Hills, AZ before passed on, he nearly a year later on Labor Day. We met in a loaded meeting nicely over a 2 week stay about life in general and religion that I wanted to found further including learning his undergrad degree was called a Spirit major at a Presbyterian college, got some Alice my mother details and his long-time wife Nancy, and tried to gain a church network I wanted.

I cherish most he said we had a lot of fun, which turned my life around as of that instance framing my mood better from when he said it. I had fun all the time with him all my life, while I was with him alone or with our family. I know he was mean when I was a child, primarily for playing football and going to the park. Adults say strict for that type of father, and with his arms in playing up warrior when I said I wanted him knight for me being worth one or higher than him. We're weird in the Rosenberg, but justice can lead to true recognition as is The Honorable Gregg Jann who is me this work's author. "Fun" busted up when I was heavy in my heart/mind without him toiling on meaningful psychology and suffering and on election Boards back home; even losing the internet and other great "larking" credits I battle for in my original invention.

Like I'm learning in repast, my voice may have been too soft for anyone else but me to hear to him all his life and his eyeballs got hugely black in his sharp advanced age when I asked if he was blinded in sex experiences like I think I was in this life. He patted my head, and I just don't know if he ever knew about the eye drops story from the girl/young woman now a mother (previous mentioned in *Van Goghing Gregg*) is true about Catholic bishop or Roman Catholic Cardinal supplying drugs for me to prepare or punish or both. I was just saying something different than be my dad's career in my occupational goal of priest spoken very young and then later in front of people in causing child priest abuse to me. – I always had ability and surely now giving me a license to talk AND write politics and religion, combining philosophy books spoken in my innocence of all crimes using mental health field innovations created in part at least by the author.

First when sex happened around 40 years old time for the first time not known immediate memory, I see and think I that I was elected on the school board always looking for more if there is more there like progressive judges, 2) now a speaking career as de-stigma presenter for a non-profit, and 3) as always ambition in getting voter support among Catholics and all for a peace theme ballot or US constitution– These needs of mine for each or many us kept me silent about "at-the-priest-abuse" from Roman Catholics and their hierarchy. They were using myself and my Reverend minister/father who is my dad or was this from one of a later group of class I talked to in Montgomery hiding harm to me rather than my original more innocent younger in age family and big family next door shirking their duty and in not so much offers of friendship not close inter-connective school-mates and dating of "Gregg's Grade."

# Chapter 2

## Notes in Kindness Leading

**Mental Health Educator/Blog Writer's Educated Mind Breaks Off**

**Insert within blogging vignette on Working Disabled Program by Gregg K. Jann cont.**

[See Chapter 2 for sample text complete suggestion by author Gregg Jann] I need you to know **"Truth to Origin"** is what I want my US Constitutional Amendment 2 or 3 paragraphs named, then signed Source Perspective Designer = not a group, spec individual Gregg K. Jann; as I bet my name gets scratched out of the copies or finished document. I have these 2 (it is just 1) written on a school district document for Character Ed that teaches soft skills that I want for teaching peace not hate crime for vocational advantage, starting with California. The other 2$^{nd}$ sent to the Publisher for my writing contract I did not see included in revised agreement writing for moot point or something status Pennsylvania ignores. I kept a copy reserving for my purposes so inclined written here. Both paragraphs are mine and are my writing as well as a third based on my invention, in CA Civil

Law some Federal jurisdiction like us copy right office why we need you, and we need people who are disabled, sick and dependent on the constitution for more love in the air – conservatively applied. To start healthy and loving Day 1 birth 0 with prenatal care, children and parents and interested adults to include: paragraph 2) **Advocacy where needed; unlimited Disabled P. Econ Rights included. Property; Safety Net Econ w/Supports and Recovery with Ownership R. not taken from Consumer; Health and Relationship Status No Discrimination in money; and Greater Author IP Rights for Monetary; 1) with Soft Skills Taught +** in school in first paragraph. Add 3) see below for in explanation victim's restitution size of alleged internet inventor of peace themes, and who are false origin business idea making money harm to origin, and just criminals hurting people that I think government trusts should pay people hurt by crime in print up of money, particularly size of internet and AIDS name stolen from Gregg K. Jann perhaps for him.

Analysis of this, non-quoted **The Jann Amendment**, copies upon request from The Honorable Gregg Jann, call me Gregg Jann, are in Chapter 5 of this *Truth to Origin* book: Designed for victory of our Humanity and making better people who may be students, and co-aligned goals of authentic economy making source rich with money not matter who the correct person is righteously. May bring into USA billions or trillions of dollars for wrongful thinking Gregg was banned from making money while he worked on the internet on Social Security. Or was just a consumer not working and otherwise productive. Author writes/teaches in Presenting for a non-profit and exemplify his own creation of 3) **Social Responsibility and Customer Service/Hold Economy** to bring him the internet or/and other tantamount good things. For example, if these get him billions of dollars, perhaps these 2 items belong on the 3<sup>rd</sup> paragraph leading banks, businesses, strangers to not hurt "you." meaning victims restitution. Do trust holding with informed consent and release more understanding with kindness objectives to client. It will also protect the environment for beyond our own group think under some manager's nose who is only interested inside the office and bottom line.

**It's a good one, Mr. President,** I say because it makes more humanity(like in psychology terminology which I don't like); counts more people who are creative, sick, and disabled, young, not just students, a place for gentle persons; builds who we are to an ideal with more understanding as I see it, and makes us money to right people who were poorer sources, and we can do justice to people who were set up false imprisonment by government in my own guilt by association by limitations with never an ability to pay it back. Note: civil codes, not criminal from Gregg K. Jann is the "Teach Peace +2 Amendment"-For Good People. People we are won't fall through the cracks socially, conservatively applied trying to limit intrusion but growing ability to teach and care out community wide– not too much interference but a stronger community that cares about the bottom rung of socio-economics and getting out of supports Upward Social Mobility way like I did work my way off disability entitlements when starting 30 years old same decade of my age receiving supports not myself or family first time.

Shyness and Anxiety I had make one falsely appear heart is uncaring, I was great in hard-nosed political debates and wanted peace not nukes, but I like people and all Presidents. I am not mean, but I don't think foreign countries would attack USA if I make headway with income and attention. Please do, recognize me for exploits I thought were hidden even if I "forgot" them from medicine, poison or not. I access Santa Rosa, CA as a former non-partisan elected official in Democratic circles turned off by Civic rudeness in performing. I can make a difference because I made legal improvements wherever I was standing willing to make history not thinking I deserve consequences.

**Note:** Governor and Mr. President: Pay me for designing CA Prop 63 MHSA 2004 and beyond, and other credits I work on at least as a lawyer-type contributor for source perspective designer. All of my articles whether just 2 or all 3 in The Jann Amendment may stop/prevent wars if we have peace on the constitution, making "Peace Say"-side money which is safe enough to talk about outside of regimented bully and sameness in society. Education is supposed to make greater income in money, so the Peace in this context does not stand alone or outside of success in talking verbally about options and where we need to go. We'll get understanding to each other and with church/religious backing to grow in religious tolerance in their rank and file membership.

Origin gets attacked and discriminated socially and for pay in employment, people use medicine poison for first and originals to steal in Capitalism and in religious persecution, and having a specialty in mental health like I work having does need workability to get in the door and then just a competent pulpit like blogs, my dot.com, and books for an audience for non-Profit Presenter is accomplished outside of great workability habits.)

**Jannda.com blog dot.com continued:** Not knowing if medicine from MDs, and work rehab supports like Department of Vocational Rehab and public employee run Medi-Cal entitlements, require forced poverty on disabled workers, no matter how smart, significant, or skilled they are like I make history.

**Question:** I did ask taking after credit card type business literature in career advice to not "follow your dreams" in activity like opening a restaurant in job applications: Do you think work supervisors rate history-making as insubordination for greater, or just a conflict of interest in financial industry acumen for struggles and ethics for change and service like the community of humans out there beyond captivity of the bank's office?

Don't confuse (12 body and 10 face as 1 average women ranker, none of these women homemakers and counseling apparatus 2nd incomes was lower than 19 ranker f and b.) having unknown sex to me in actual with my history. Law tell me I invented a legal status of "forced technical virgin" in Sonoma County as I'm legal and my 3 prior books prove I didn't see all of the incident at the Pt. Reyes bluff before I was ever stricken mentally ill and never was I in Special Ed. i.e. I placed the word "encourage" in a labor union contract and a school district contract– so I did make business history by including a dissociated class of workers in an article for a less hurt, marginalized group of workers who are counselors in case those employers who want them will do better handling in kindness for their future goals than I received.

The System kept me from working in Case Management, and I never had a CM for decades before Capgrass Transference hit me recommended for group attendance only not one on one. CM as an area is ripe for reform, for I read at CSU, Chico it is illegal to manipulate the environment; which was a treasure trove of ethical intellect while I lived in the dorms while hurt. I wanted US President Reagan to say this on TV and sales sheets of paper as we were marketing "shoe phones" or what turned out to be called cell phones.

As I see Persons with Disabilities Econ Rights worth on constitution and on DNC "questionnaire" surveys perhaps aided by

Gregg K. Jann's input. I do need a 2nd paragraph below Teach Peace within Character Education, as any of our people not having full rights, and we can title the whole article **Truth to Origin** signed openly Source Perspective Designer with my name scratched off for the ages. I do have one and another that I won't muck up here, but et al. Seemed like I needed inclusive of my writing style and background materials as I am a lonely influence. I am a Big Love to care hidden from me to survive enemy rockets in my imaginary war gaming since college for real.

Medicine might cycle harm to consumer employees intentionally to show who is boss and with low or no regard to people who are not a doctor but doctors like the struggle of working. I built union ability to possibly fight for workers' longevity if consumers too and we'll see how I win by lonely at the top with nothing to lose and caring with social responsibility mine not belonging to academia. Chico State would be proud, but I'm not yet rich for no credit except through my intelligence and innovation and creative writing filed at copyright.gov published)

**Blog of dot.com:** With each job transition, sometimes it is good to use trainings to expand mind for work. Ask for education in negotiations. Accepting less pay may be understood if a more rural region on the outskirts of the financial center.

This blog **Jannda.com** was responding to a low pay opportunity, no money job training opportunity which declined me for caring about my deceased mother in a peer counseling question about loss that wasn't long before. I keep my dignity with other judgements adding to my wisdom, for "no pearls before swine" as they don't respect at Wellness Center, Interlink, and other communist hotbeds of out of towners Goodwill employs. I said the Bible in structured walk through and my quotes originally to

me in larking beauty in way that got into this book of Jesus para-
bles from either my mother, father, or churchly background they
went to. For my good management planning including designs
of the Mental Health Services Ace, all I got was un fairly Gay
Surround and sexual harassment of the worst degree from
"rapish" women and worst type of verbal rudeness from gay men
at one lunch space I helped to invent. Its wrongful to surround
somebody of one of any type not his own, which should be a law
working for Gregg Jann particularly in his home town where he
is a hero unknown.

*Property Rights and Ethics*

## Prescription for Schizophrenia late teens -early 20s

As you may recall from earlier reading or my non-profit presen-
tations, I was first stricken with "schizophrenic thinking
processes" in a "prodromal" schizophrenia period of not seeking
help from 18 ½ years old until going to the doctors just before
22 years old. I kept silent of my mental problems and did not tell
anyone for a secret held to me: for fear of treatment, the stigma
of surrounding people, and the loss of financial support from family and the administration at my first 2 colleges. I was able to
graduate with having a track record of academic success so-so and
need to achieve with the medication provided that solved my
basic health issue stated by my main psychiatrist of concentration
and memory.

Throughout my 20s and some into my 30s I danced the night
away 4 nights each week, asking boldly young women to dance.
I did not go further in social experience in the dating life, and intentionally abstained from sexual relations and more than one
beer each night I went dancing to prove to no one watching that

I wasn't an alcoholic. I was crazy and running my game trying for these women to ask me out or at least for my phone number, and to take steps toward me. Imagine that.

My business degrees helped by not prodding into feelings and requiring no empathy in answers. We learned systems, particularly computer MIS, and knowing to respect was before college. I was almost all responsible with cash handling paperboy and church custodian work experience each over one year long as a youth, and writing published editorials to go along with degree from junior college. I was captain of intramural flag football team at Chico. I had bad routine, was unaware personally, and hid socially from female conversations not men friends as defense mechanism to not be discovered or committed for grandiose ideas. I was not delved into deeply by students who may have wondered about that rare project deadline missed, or that maybe one assignment miscue. I did get written up 3 times in successive nights by just one R.A. for loud music in my solo room last semester, when I always blared my rock music to no head phones. Today I tell audiences I feel very inconsiderate about my listening habits back when I was in my 20s, and I never took it for granted just didn't know anybody minded. I read classic novels on my own from the library, and learned my depth and perceptions about people from the literature as best I could have done.

I filled my goals, which meant a lot to my political ambition. Looking back now, it might not seem like much to onlookers to zenith at elected school board member and Innkeeper for a political club. I can keep my hand in politics, and get more active with knowledge I have learned about the process and get acquainted with the Younger crowd to help achieve a state and Federal constitution amendment as you can read in Chapter 5. My themes are consistent throughout my editorial copy and election statements as I governed for greater kindness among our children to spread peace and authenticity in our economy later.

After college graduations and writing printing letters worth in my mind a paper trail for the US Supreme Court like Conscientious Objector legal status if I wanted to pull it out like I always wanted to be part of a "Peace Formula" of making the World Wide Web or Internet, I got a job in management in San Francisco. Jostling about for independence grew from the college town with a roommate mostly, and I lived alone in a studio after a one-week failure in an Oakland hotel. This - year management trainee work stint provided lots of warm regard at work with me a focus point of smiles and attention – I was not heavy handed in personnel and in fact avoided scheduling employees, written discipline, and worked with my employees and did not bump up to Senior Assistant Manager like I did by not doing sexual harassment of any kind.

Once laid off, I felt an "aneurism" or something dizzy and light headed to make me not look for work on my own. I asserted to my mother I needed to live with her, and she provided container emotional support in providing a home living with her. I did not play around with booze or women, and on this other hand do not know to this day how she kept the house so clean.

I worked long hours, and still to this day as a writer/politico. I worked hard, particularly in the 90s as a community activist filling in political goals as a volunteer and then after working some years as a group home counselor I worked 100-hour weeks including driving a truck for 70 hours each week for a year and a half. I was out to prove we consumers can work hard, that suffering was like being uncomfortable at working long hours, and that I individually was responsible even if the pay to me was not.

Today I write, and go to groups, and get educated. I take time with family who are my sisters. I have the first time in my life a chance to relax from overwork overload of stress, and reach the stars in trying to reclaim IP that I feel was taken and stolen from me.

I enjoy church and the local Sonoma County area, and the nearby attractions. It is like I am on a more pedestrian pathway of life, almost in retirement, but I do head banging philosophy for the day we want non-violence taught in schools with something I know and want – like disabled income and property rights not taken away by a Safety Net security, with of course Victims Restitution article for as the previous RA stated – the Biggest One Wins.

# Chapter 3

## Summer Heat Tucked Inside

### High School and College Grads of Family
Submitted on Thu, 2017-06-08 13:49

Be sure to send "congratulations" to graduates in your family, from siblings to nieces and nephews. If you can afford it, a little money not minute add up with others. I'm not about cash, instead maybe self-reveal for minor "heads up" without genetics tie in.

Advice you know about, generalizations or platitudes, praises about deserving for their hard work, and wishing good luck and more success in their future need to be communicated from trusted sources. In person visits might be embarrassed to say such things, so cards may be more embellished than phone calls.

*Family and Friends*

### A former formal liaison to 2 bad sides
Submitted on Sat, 2017-06-24 14:24

Medicine punishes. It's not always directly related to the disease condition, and psychiatry knows this out of hand. Behavior correction by counselors is unethical if done chemically. This is wrongful if medically induced by doctors and higher up therapists.

Those who want too much younger wives and girlfriends is one un-Americanism enforced by doctors' care. Like Gregg touched 20 somethings unknown to him -he funded all their world. 29 years olds for more square may be needed to stop doctor hurting him, for example flapping agitated, no energy, and outdoors incontinence. In which these were just said to get community support for a trial in comments to Doctors, and not an exact complaint rap sheet bringing on more side effects.

*Property Rights and Ethics*

### *Van Goghing Gregg*: Hon Jann de-draft Europe?
Submitted on Sat, 2017-07-08 17:30

Summer reading is accurate about blurbs spread to afar from a joyful youth of author Gregg Jann in *Van Goghing Gregg: Recovery Toward Love*. An incident Mr. Jann had with family/friends came to him in re-memory psychiatric drug therapy as a former counselor/current MH Instructor/blogger may have helped open up more Golden Gate National Recreation Area across the bay from San Francisco, CA. We at Jannda.com and United Kingdom can read his essay posted on Amazon.uk.co, and his latest review getting the word out on *Bettering the World* to determine justly he bravely helped to de-draft Europe.

Gregg Jann's back pack party particularly may have made Pt Reyes National Seashore safer to do so at Gregg's sacrifice (and his friend - no contact) and his later journey into MH consumerism. "They" don't tell you these things, and author did call the Ranger recently in today's era at Pt. Reyes Station or was it Sheriff's substation for help in clues, which author did not follow up in looking up files except brainstormed.

Movie here with his being the winning party is what motivated Gregg in escaping danger alone as a 15 year old boy while a nearby high school sophomore. That Trail Side Strangler was incredibly ugly in murder spree crimes and Mr Gregg Jann was blithely unaware and am only hazy about what Gregg did in response in this True, nonfiction book in chapter One. The Honorable Gregg Jann said a lot of great political philosophy religion things in his early life. Later Chico State was the right college for him in business for economics personhood not used up by US President Reagan except for his taking speeches.

Not quite in *Van Goghing Gregg*, but worth considering for philosophy why me books: Criminology without Gregg in a trial for religious persecution by Marin Sheriff is one theory of poisoned mental illness, along with taking value worth starting of inventing computer internet and also blocking outspoken peace flower president in campaigning as a SRJC student.

The publisher Rose Dog Books also categorizes *Van Goghing Gregg: Recovery Toward Love* to be autobiography/religion & philosophy/economics - Gregg stops a Marin mass murderer conspiracy cult, discusses Reconciling Methodist theological aspects, reveals he was initially early in Global Warming theory as an inspiration, and educates us on the Safety Net economy in these pages like he did as an econ degree in college. Included is a tribute to a movie star he may have helped to invent if she is a troupe while Gregg was in a IP lawyer's office unknown to what his problem was with his phantom girlfriend next door in working life and Gregg Jann gives thanks these people.

*Family and Friends*

## Reminiscing on People There

Submitted on Wed, 2017-07-26 14:00

Enjoyably remembering the past is healthy, particularly in the presence of others who were there. Facebook.com is great to include written synopsis sometimes with pictures of events, childhood teams, and similar current vacation spots among those who knew you from past even youth.

It is vital to keep in touch if broken spirited or lonely due to MH recovery. I don't see a lot of persons with serious mental illness take part in FB due to internet blockage and any zombieness in get out and go.

*Family and Friends*

## New People inside Bible for 55th B-Day

Submitted on Sat, 2017-08-05 13:56

As a minister's son I feel compelled that some people feel left out of the bible. Women coming to the forefront after struggle, Gays getting rights like not before, and my MH consumer journey with success through positions in government and health care seem fit the times for more relevancy. School and business too, all told I'm a provider.

People with disabilities differ in health needs, recovery methods and outlook vary, and the illnesses suffered are constraining to the heart in formats not understood cookie cutter approach. I'm still waiting for my female girlfriend after 25 years of regular membership & attendance at church.

*Holistic Community and Permaculture*

## Gregg Likes Feminism if as Kind as Him

Submitted on Sat, 2017-08-26 13:50

I'm a nice type of person, and was guarded as kindness is taken advantage of if not toughly defended. I see "soft skills" like I invented while elected after I wrote editorial copy for school inclusion ahead of the US Equal Rights Amendment now in my adult advocacy for another Constitution Amendment; I talked to Marin to Oregon Congressman 1-1 in person at Democlub.org and the staff of my own years ago in his Santa Rosa office.

Malala Yousafzai's winning a prior year's Nobel Peace Prize proves women rights in education is an important freedom of intellect and for work. She survived attempted murder starting with blog writing in Pakistan under the Taliban in 2009. It was the same the year I finished publishing my 1st book and after I started this MH blog also under ban I should consider.

*Advocacy*

## Does USA Like Their Champions?

Submitted on Wed, 2017-09-06 16:58

Mental Health Consumers, former volunteers then workforce 10-year steady after management career, union negotiators now sole proprietorship, disabled worker off entitlements all of them for a time: do people ever appreciate ADVOCATEs walking the walk trying for Upward Social Mobility based on their own talent and ingenuity while I may have made the most econ history and elections?

No emotional support like introductions to a wife, no recognition of meritorious medal, no economic reward for home ownership for all I did intellectually with sweat equity by working overload.

*Advocacy*

## Who Loves You on Web Search Engines

Submitted on Mon, 2017-09-11 15:47

[Does anybody wonder if this below insight dated 9/11 written exactly Central Mountain time brought on the fire strike a month later in our town of Santa Rosa, CA? I first heard from a Washington Mutual investment broker as I was shopping my retirement account, that he used Jockularity tone in seeming to say only Roman Catholics could invest in the internet according to Microsoft and the Seattle group of old money in their industrial families. Approved by the US Senate? This bank visit was near 2005 and I forgot about it like a "forced technical virgin" with hazy memory, and perfect deniability by set up witness coworker as I returned later asking for confirmation of this highlight. I once interviewed for Sonoma Business newspaper/magazine and didn't think I could handle the job as reporter/fact gatherer as I lacked a lot of focus. My Jewish friend probably pierced my veil with his bad reputation word to remind me of the tough fight on my hands. I for "Peace Say" and internet glory I had in mind for my college major and work, including ideals for un-Pirating Western Economy and advocating Safety Net Economy without discrimination to Gregg K. Jann to replace communism for more freedom and greater business]

Blog continuing:

A sign wanting a relationship suddenly occurred to this owner to put into the web search engine, "Do Any Women Like Gregg Jann." I've been single and wanted to get married once my health set in. I was taken advantage of and punished during or by M therapy for not being married already. It's like being "Not Catholic" as the reasons for firing for my salary and wage jobs letting me go or internet companies, others keeping me away from work I designed as source perspective designer as a Protestant Religious symbol man. All my 6 top notices on web were dry and said something.

*Family and Friends*

**Note:** I did sound un-Catholic in this book like I never have been, in my entire life; just here in context of stolen internet and economic discrimination in employment leading to the life of. It was a sudden realization in my thoughts, from when I was working on the internet and asked my dad for help from him in New York with me in Chico State dorm room, me sick, and that I was surrounded by a type of people of that other religion even them stating one time hazy, "we're Stealing Catholic the Olde Way." I'm sorry my father didn't seem much to help me. To "Creedence" perhaps in the Department of Defense, I'm sorry for wanting to fill a hole in a lack we had in the Northwest for Reagan's Rose-Colored Glasses home of the H-bomb besides test field. I worked on the internet while a student and peace themes later too, and someone used their group for an administration era Presidential Ban for speech writer significance no less from Gregg Jann. Only Catholics and Jesuits would take everything from someone and later call the Knight, an American elected official former, one of their Saints. It seems a life path me not of my Protestant religion except PRS and Gregg K. Jann.

The constitution amendment I want, we deserve, and those of other elements owe the USA of us has nothing but try to abate hate crime and all of the crimes, and help honest make a more economy, and heal better. Cults stealing from way back when? Reagan using by choice Catholic to steal the internet?

**Reader:** Look into this and it does take a sense of inner Affirmative Action and **Truth to Origin** Amendment by Gregg K. Jann to correct this in economy. AA was in a headline I did not read the article of, and it was good in spurring thinking in Trump's Time for Mr. President said it. I didn't like Reagan for hurting permanent things about people; like college funding which blocked opportunities lasting a lifetime, the environment he detested, and human rights opposition. This Far Right of his presidency could have used one group on purpose for the internet development, and try his damnedest to make it a monopoly. No more for data security, privacy, and integrity to credit wisely the right men and women inventers including philosopher of peace for all us to the world.

## Vietnam War PBS Television Series is Worth It
Submitted on Fri, 2017-09-29 13:46

Covering my fandom for my favorite Emmy nominated Actress name game? (Shailene). My own invention of "Information Therapy" is usefully gained counseling care by scanning web, television, newscasts even paper, asking questions. Trying to make whole with critical thinking and feeling with empathy, made better with people-relating like conversation.

The Vietnam War on PBS series fills holes I had as born in 1962. I learned details about the bombing. I also grew well for the soldiers. I again appreciated 2 Conscientious Objector stories, and seeing protest was nationwide not just Cal Berkeley. I was formed by churches, M*A*S*H, and media hyper Patriotic as I visited the recruiter at college grad time in '86.

*Property Rights and Ethics*

## Safety, Fire, and the Department of Peace Building
Submitted on Sat, 2017-10-14 18:41

Asking your Congressmen to Cosponsor HR 1111 to establish the US Department of Peace Building may need Heroes and Dollars. The founder of Jannda.com designed the Mental Health Services Act which passed our electoral process in November 2004.

Gregg stopping 70s Marin mass murderer The Trailside Strangler in Pt Reyes may have opened up a National Recreation Area. Advocating safety and Character Ed in soft skills while elected at Piner-Olivet USD may have spread to the community. Ending the spread of Santa Rosa's Tubbs fire gratefully at the school district boundary?

*Homeland into Foreign Policy*


## Mono Culture and Fire Created by the Moneyed
Submitted on Wed, 2017-11-01 21:52

The North Bay fires of October 2017 leaving 20,000 thousand homeless looked like an Act of God/multi warhead bomb attacking. Santa Rosa and the Napa Co. answered with noted love in the air. Doctors are misanthropes about birds like ordinary jerks.

If principle attacked us, One Point re-joiner is to dislike concentration of wealth and disproportionate distribution of income in wineries, Napa, and Fountain Grove? Answer for econ liking: Change EIRs to discourage Mono Culture of cultivating all only one crop which drives away items making the North Bay special, harming birds that fly and walk.

*Holistic Community and Permaculture*

**A Small Business Owne**r doesn't know the "2 Schwan Men in a Truck" joke as he was never told it or will be last in a crowd to know it. I drove alone with training. (70 hours each 5-day week, some more, and most weeks at least on average one shift at the group homes just employment to keep my toe in in Mental Health. Difference of opinion about MH consumer rights took Gregg K. Jann to fight and struggle for them, succeeding in his authoring that class of counselor's employment rights on labor contract. History-making I do like plan and am successful in designing the tax act of the MHSA, as I tell you normally. I've been worth Saint in the Roman Catholic Church when you include my school board goal on non-violence and general emotional well-being taught to students vocationally, some others like larking AIDS and what all my books say. I am not a catholic, name me now when you do and pay immediately now, pay me money and return to this American the money stolen – a plan I can use for peace to go along with the Jann Amendment. Bring the prettiest women to the Saintly Knight for his comeuppance and money to Gregg K. Jann, free of encumbrances.)

I don't know what made the fires look crazy all at once going toward downtown when I wrote an award application for my Book III for publicity as hero in the area for good vibes me and Victims. Nor surmising who/what blew up the fast food restaurants I wasn't supposed to go to after Check In group that made me feel like I won the fire struggle along with my packing and hosting my family member over her worry. It looked like a gas line, but my un-expert analysis lacks experience and the Home Construction class in Montgomery High School was cut from the school's budget with state services of Jarvis/Gann's Prop 13. Those who force no property value enthusiasm can supposition wrongness from evil hearts of man toward Gregg K. Jann, them in a lawyer's costume once a raw form of greater humanity through Acts of God set in from above and they see they, themselves are guilty.

Houses blackened and flattened right next to schools and some schools destroyed, 24 casualties, scene destroyed looked like almost heard half tranced in sleepy drugged state **"Geronimo"** yelled or screamed, Man of the Sky falling, warning a bomb of fire and atom even leveled houses 8 mile strip touching and encompassing one school boundary where I was board member meaning peace in curriculum and stretching to rival districts not well meaning to them of those of money and low budget behind that hospital – it touched all classes of our people in total desertion and destruction. I stayed and wrote this book, kept up the blog writing, and kept up my groups' attendance and added my bible study presentation for Legends of peace making. I helped create Woolsey with "left" essay publicly printed then published in Bettering the World after reprint at Santa Rosa Democratic Club – people knew me even if moving on these days like high school. You got to know who's important. Help me find a wife and my money (2 things), credit more, and even more for Medal and Movies if able are worth my regard to me. Why bomb Santa Rosa Northern Flank for mistreatment of a cold warrior who meant Russian refusenik and peace treaty holder for our creator for his own money to pass the US Senate upon negotiation? I didn't tell them or anybody crazy in DC or anywhere clients are. Don't rape me like girls do White Fright or something in Military parlance, and provide relationship for nice love from a woman and to this guy author who finds himself to marry a pretty lady looks inside and outside morals everywhere.

The people did not approach me about injustices economically applied individually screwing someone who needed to be rich for Lordly talent in history-making in the USA, and the bully is on its heels whether it be US Military proper, just rich fat cats from states like Seattle thieves, or homeowners that aren't much for churches or charity like I try on subsistence hopefully past. Are we fighting Seattle pay dirt, or 'Enola Gay Gimme' for stealing me and being given computer IP design? Check here in this non-fiction book. Its time they paid me Gregg K Jann after a life of middle class niceness to my siblings and their offspring who had them.

In these fires' aftermath I heard schizophrenia voices inside my head like never before going over a hard manuscript editing details as a symptom of stress and common to schizophrenia. It was brought on by a mean guy eating rudely making vulgar sounds where I was working in supposedly quiet public study. Some psychologist could have instigated that, for me saying something similar to last time I told my mother I recovered. Those "healthy, recovered, don't need you" sounding words going into the ears of therapists are known to more regular client culture to give brain pain or greater symptoms, at least temporarily, intentionally as industry psychology practice of mental health profession because of why. They are a "you know what" in meanness. – I didn't commit a crime, raised money for mental health care, in a tax ballot initiative for CA and am accomplished mostly for safety for schools. I never heard voices in my inner head before from schizophrenia symptoms.

Religious persecution for advocating corrections of "truths" which were standard lies about origins and who owns told many times like Nazi's can be a "buddy prompt" for my good, hard work in writing God and man, so you reporters to medicine are false and shall be condemned if you think I deserve badness. I didn't make anybody homeless, and helped stop the spread of fire by safety policy in a community I was responsible for by making it my Piner-Olivet school governance team's business. I was mostly about school shootings on campus and not using barb wire around school – I care like a depressing social worker and make up prevention brainstorms.

It's not a lot of traditional success I have, without money. I win everything when in court, so the law does barriers to entry. DON'T TAKE WHAT I GOT LIKE A COMMUNIST SOLDIER OR JAIL BOY. Am I too good for Church sermons handed down for the ages? A mankind lesson on making do and changing the course of evil in USA/world if such were to happen? Mortally wounded and sacrificed emotionally for disease recovery research based on my word choices and body language? Capitulate, chemical-using bully, and pay Gregg K. Jann and suck a donkey's dick if my rich woman assignment for the right and privilege of existence in this Land.

Now I write on a mental health services blog with a health license and trademark in mental health. I don't think in my theocratic manner that women like openness, restructuring, and more moral that solved our cold war in mental health manner before Putin, which is the work since of Mr. Gregg Kevin Jann. I don't know what a girlfriend relationship would be like. I want one, or several before I get to marry a female. The doctor knows I work down there, which means biologically operational how I say it. Work and lectures get a load of bullies from the US Military or just plain you know what's from Big City like the Apple. I try for privacy but you see, I strive with some things to work on. I'm happy, and I am usually not the most talkative fellow.

Also re: fire pulling it out of me, things just seemed too weird in pictures that restaurant part of destruction with trees standing. Psychiatry Department in the most expensive section of Santa Rosa on the high hills overlooking Our Town does cause suspicion for those concerned with US Piracy of the Consumer. It is but a theory not shown on the boob tube as Industrial Black Out as Industrial Policy of business and government. I read about industrial policy in facto economic organizations regionally or throughout the nation during college. For example, the racket of all internet founders and wives Catholic wrongfully compared to economy fair distribution not using good American Affirmative Action to be inclusive in secret deal not told to me and hurting me in gainful employment.

I was never able to work in a computer field like my college education except I designed work and peace, it was brought to my attention I had relationship discrimination in employment not just locally to Sonoma County, and that employers do often not pay volunteers once in or even board members good same industry or on job application. Rackets in preventing freedom through commerce for an Idea Man who stood running for US President like he was one is how I look at things, with my ability to create words and create care for people.

I know power lines are dangerous, obstructive trees catch sparks that spread, and I know wind can be powerful for normal explanations among the defendant industry. So are trucks capable of running over wood poles, and no suicide is appropriate support for the real/reel internet inventor for what a book author later Marquis Who's Who member said to his Sales Supervisor as the Schwan Man worked too hard for a disabled recovery who quit school board election to drive and sell with the truck. My company of JannDA.com has a brainstorming creativity investigative thought process on inner works of the environment good for myths and also debunking the current Pablum forced on you by the TV and most media for my critical thinking ability on my own. "Don't make it up" is not the only rule for criminal justice worth war. We don't want you to spread rumors, or make panic, or cause crime against people and property, or harm recovery efforts. Or be racist and prejudicial.

I think I heard there were lots of fires in Germany before they started WWII. Things got me to thinking, after a late night to bed hearing with unsuspecting unconcern wind moving my blinds and sirens around the Square below. I fell asleep as Emergency was happening, turned on the TV and heard no big deal just about Napa fire and turned it off. I was groggy overnight and almost fell off my bed. I woke up at 9:00am that first Monday, 15 minutes later getting a call from family that called earlier to no signal not getting through the phone line.

This work of my non-fiction book is just opportunism on a peace elected officials part not treason but a better idea than destruction with foreign policy on his mind homebound glory. Kind of like escapism they say Hollywood is, "recovery realism" to get to honest life story from similar details on mind for psychosis treatment from counseling this to myself, a published author.

On this other hand of critical thinking brainstorming investigation or "recovery realism", both non-fiction to detail: I was a cover-up by business and government. Fill in the blanks after reading my career and knowing I'm honest. We can pay Gregg Jann and make this no longer delay and take it so it can look natural by Gregg who is this author if the government print up money for his pay to reach him soon without encumbrances and without restriction. I do an innovation thing with nude credits after a computer education with a mental health services trademark. I don't have much friends that are close while I spend most of my time in church and politics for over 25 years same places. I'm in Land of Bull Shit in Town Known for Bad Pussy – It's the women, the men who love them, and those of the wrong hole. I told a lawyer stepping out of his office that.

Presenter was made to look nervous by medicine side effect when Trump as Candidate said I. I didn't hear him say that hate crime in ridiculing a journalist as I don't think I'm a journalist as I have a health business license and try peace as a businessman/philosopher. I wasn't certain of an avowed murderer in prison for life during a performance for his nonprofit work when the inmate had what I believe to be a stencil tattoo. I thought later it looked like a map outline shown on TV of the Napa/Sonoma North Bay Fires in post reflection

*It added up for stealing one internet inventor, other things too from one person if we count my speaking, writing, and developing nude credits more than in classes. Some credits of mine designed with my educated ability, who is "Eyiou"/me/GKJ for meaning more than money as in religion, environment, and peace themes all my life including movies maybe songs. This includes new words that are cute, needed to fill a hole, and New York resident experiences. I was treated badly by psychiatry as much as oppression and as a chemical induced prisoner near sex slavery obsession and given no female to hold like I would love her for my wife.*

*An Act of God wishing to Honor Gregg Jann as a former elected community activist owed money by the government for designing the MHSA 2004, and other things. For 18 ½ years old first stricken, maybe poisoning to 55 YO and continuing when I want recovery and*

*to heal immediately. I was always never jailed or hospitalized or in a court trial charged with crime. This medicine punishment/just consequences must stop and it's time to start the reward for economic "larking" credits which must begin for the source perspective designer who is Gregg K. Jann.*

*[I'm innocent of fire, both these and any other destroying houses. You who are pretty female together with me with from inside my pants, and my political messaging for originally spoken words known to honest sources is opportunistic for me. I am sorry for what happens to victims, and not all strangers are sad for what happens to others. I am sorry for the civic rudeness. I was in a wall of silence for 50 years since I entered kindergarten at Village Elementary and said opening the door 1ˢᵗ time, "I'm from Nebraska." Something going back to childhood with the preacher's son; which kept friends, lovers, and my economic projects away.*

*[I send off materials, email included, for book awards for my past public service & heroism current policy effects as fire raged toward downtown at the bank while I wore a mask writing without editing an application. I worked on winning the Award for more attention of the Wine Country for all Sonoma/Napa does receive, in example it was just one evening broadcast with the ABC World News TV starring Anchor in town which is remarkable.]*

It wasn't me at all who did anything about creating the North Bay Fires like conspiracy or arson or mistake prone like mail boxes accidentally. I like birds and enjoy them having habitat particularly right near us like Spring Lake. I want community leaders, not rich stooges who don't contribute to general kindness for the surroundings, in our cities' grand homes. Doctors are fine. I'm not a criminal except willing to be a court Plaintiff for recovery with and when funding available as I write and advocate fairly for improvement. It should be just me for certain accounts. I may be known by many people in politics and customers and readers and people who are friends.  The money to win I want to go to Gregg K. Jann, not the birds, but don't destroy their habitat because bird life is beautiful and doesn't cheat.

I don't know if "guano", bird doo, is more harmful than flushing too many meds down. But in Sonoma County our heritage means love animals and birds that are wild life.  And certainly not out of towners coming here developing land to their own purposes perhaps treading on our innovators who may not always agree with Washingtonians, Republicans in office, or the Far Right in past existence.

When I was a kid I thought the New Yorkers, others were stalkers threatening local Santa Rosa, even if not especially me from corruption. One not Nancy was a professional life wrecker to divorce my father to take her away, because my mother loved Sonoma and Dad wanted to work in a huge city like LA. NYC was great for him in career. I guess things had to be done, but don't lie about my step mom for 25 years who is Nancy Hearn or who or who not my relations are like somebody "poisoned the well" against me in 9th grade.

No, I don't appreciate no time but buying candy at Kmart together by Reverend Father when I was a child and no talk at Presbyterian Churches USA to me, which was group effort in regular no caring. My mom moved us there to a church across town as an "Exodus", to Methodist. I don't know if/how my life story designed Reconciling Methodist from not-"Gay" rough, rogue teenager just talking priesthood only liking female who were not present, to Conscientious Objector legal case just contingency if I wanted to use it ,with draft counseling at church; and in school statements even SRJC newspaper printed; to going inside all-recruiters station and talking to all branches of military at college graduation time for a career application at job time; already documented in books and blogs at my dot.com.

That act, recruiter et al even maybe a Russian "refusenik" somewhere reached, was proud and surprising for someone looking for a career in vicissitudes of changing America and its meaning. I not even knowing Business Casual dress code from the silence I got from peer students from high school through colleges three eventually each all total playing isolation game. You'd have to say my freedom of speech paid a dear price of income and bodily harm to someone me, and we changed those things of my involvements in design. On constitution Amendment of "Teach Peace +2" place protect children and our students who are young from marauder's IP, theft chemical disabling, and giving freedom to associate in our beliefs as civilians leading this nation. For these bad guys do bullying with intent to replace the harm that if not already happened to themselves or they're chicken from worry what will happen to them and its best it will happen to the next guy they can find.

Was some true you-know-what going to stab my foot with a knife or did wreck a tire because he/she couldn't talk like I would have confused him or her wanting advocacy on the constitution; group home or like barracks to gang bang female rape a straight white male for not playing "soldier" on the field all the way real serious like because I was an elected reporter/editorial writer; put me in paramilitary prison(The Mental Health System volunteer service private paid or me) for lackadaisical in my duties not revealing I'm a MH consumer to work or any position not ever for years because I'm not irreligious not to your confidentiality breach; or [Court Martial] me knowing stigma fires and the Lord needs me to grow your understanding of caring and non-belligerence as a not yet paid church guy of my mind cooperating.

I say and write that I know I'm a hero and was always confident I use good judgement if I ever killed someone. And no crime committed by Gregg K. Jann in my life, never an inmate of any type. I relied on my dad in absence and not churches except one employer although I go for discussions. Church one, Bible study the other to worship. However, looking at some unknown; USA churches hurt me, in my eyes during uncertain sex acts to me, Law did not help with defeat that they knew discriminations or the cult at The Bluff.  Pay me you Army the cash of my credits full glory and money to Mr. Gregg K. Jann and introduce me to wife material I want to meet, make love, and marry in just a few.

Times while former publicly elected in education and advocating character morals (attributed by certain nefarious elements in Superintendents chair wrongfully to a different US President, also wrongly than then CA Governor later President who might get Scott up in space; see later) were number one priority to get a beautiful wife not yet here. I didn't receive in my psychology reservoir in my lifetime health socially what I wrote best for students in my observations and awareness in reflection. One) I played sports during breaks and 2) I was socially caring in big manner toward the greater good and you can read my Social Responsibility essay in *Van Goghing Gregg*. To author albeit with consumer rights wanted on the Constitution according to Gregg for more humanity with econ rights who are persons with disabilities including mentally.

**On the fire tangential topic, you may see me a bigger guy, not too rambling God Forbid:** Gregg believes he said "Mono Culture" original to him first than anybody else in facto as an issue he was concerned about in running for Santa Rosa City Council while a CSU, Chico Student one summer at 21st year birthday in New City, New York. He may have got into this bar in New York City saying this verbally first geographic exact location undeclared? It was my verbal copy *right@Gregg* Jann. **Are we fighting for verbal copy rights so that we recognize innovation, building someone, and a group sense of honesty for someone's fire fight of the North Bay Fires of October in 2017.** It has to do with Gregg K. Jann and his part of the AIDS before his internet peace work, some money should come to author for disease naming.

There is the definition of Mono Culture, and also it to the conversation in which he introduced this term meant his own Napa/Sonoma County area and what would he do with his money, and specifically what did he care about? Question 2 wasn't a topical question but a piercing inquiry. I wanted to make out with a brunette but did not, she did want to but I wasn't sure how to proceed. 21 and still no known touching (to this day.)– Amazing and I didn't mean to be an untouchable like India from India or too rough, too much like Vatican for Protestant religious symbol for 475 men. I want a wife, didn't say I always did for self-fight. They get me ugly on Computer Dating, not for me. I am worth someone great because I have high Inherent Value and make up words and copy righting a peace plan as a former elected official in Santa Rosa as a white man.

One of the two women who drove author Gregg K. Jann from his father's house on Glen Haven Dr. said we're "MPs" after I said "Mono Culture" inside the bar, and I didn't let on I wanted to make up the internet in designing it originally or do my peace plans for it was dangerous to do so. This above word of "mono culture" is something for them to hear to credit me as a gift to them for them to appreciate and help if remember me build honest authenticity in economy for us and nation's economies. I was friendly and hid my unstable "hurtness" always still graduating all colleges enrolled. I was making the World Wide Web programming and connections possible as a commercial, research, and connectivity thing itself operating in the US and also in the world. I was broad in interests as a trained systems analyst with poly sci. editorials published regionally meant globally, and wanted more than money not less money and am a practical Christian philosopher for it.

Getting back to the bar we went to, it was the first time I ordered wine and maybe the first bar I went into, and I salute the two women who were there bringing me a taste of East Coast social life in person.

Later when I was still unquestioned-to-me chaste going to bars in Chico and Santa Rosa 4 times each week, I drank one beer a night (normal quickly) to prove I wasn't an alcoholic. No one was watching or cared much like I was planning to be like a Cold Warrior worth discriminating, alone in a nursing home bed at end of life with nobody. I don't want that any more or any time sacrifice my life and never meant to give up a lady who would be my wife. It just may be an element part of sacrifice that I wasn't told to not do until later by Bible Study and I always wanted a visitor-friend in person and a wife and to talk convincing if I wanted children.

I asked adult girls/women to dance, and you can add up 4 different successes spread over the hours of listening to good music each night. I didn't get your name that one night I had a chance, and I was open to you talking with me or maybe you have a daughter I can know in today's era. I didn't socialize easily back then except for hard politics and of course fucking wasn't done my insert as I wanted a nice wife not a one-night stand, and I couldn't talk conversationally with you not assertively participating.

I was running my game, which was She had to come to me and approach me. This isn't done with new gender roles just in a new era transgender biology but NO- women won't be forward maybe 6 ultimate times in their life to shy, stranger men or a much older man who conquered the world on no money fighting like a legal warrior and knight.  I wasted a lot of time being shy and nervous hardly talking to people in their raunchy mode and rarely asked for their phone number except twice or so looking for a nice person who was straight heterosexual female in Santa Rosa, CA.

# Chapter 4

## Screwed for Talking or Not, Both Originally

**"It's me, female sweetie. I'm non-fiction Author & former elected official.**

**I have a whole family to work on. Holiday with family. Or we work on movie at my place. Sole proprietor is Gregg K. Jann."**

I am a Good Man and Honest; have an education during this MIS era of mid 1980s some beyond; was brave in wanting peace making output known-talk first and newspaper-writing published editorials second; and paid a freedom price developing better-ness emotionally for you, me, and others; and economically discriminated for speaking **"safety net economy."** It was just as theory I was working on out of thin air just talking to some "Johnson" in Whitney Hall dorms, more on this later. The dialog name of above this chapter is my feeling, whenever I should be called into action on topic of safety net economy. I always said to place my trade paperback books from Dorrance Publishing by any of their imprints into your underwear drawer, for I started ending the conscription of soldiers, tried to start the new chastity, and I was just dogged all my life. I earned the right to say and publish phrases with an education and my creative type personality. I wasn't one on it nor did I ever expect to live in that state of being as long as corruption as it till present at least.

In October 2017 I say to honor a change in season for attention with caring to inventor and innovators money or not yet paid, I saved my home town from burning completely in a fire by my legacy part time public service career reserving all other rights for example religion, property, right to associate to Gregg Jann; I wanted Conscientious Objector/Commanding Officer Company of fire fighters (who could be salesmen or so in volunteer brigade like the Superintendent at my board role service time) to come up from the Bay Area to fight the flames if necessary in closed session planning dream-on as back up. I wasn't supposed to talk about revealing here about safety and volunteerism in contingency. Later to be worth remuneration for a Secret Life for Character Ed and morals.

## Why Now This?

(I think I invented the television program *Secret Life of the American Teenager* talking to my IP lawyer on the phone or in his office paid time by Jannda (trademark I filed with him long ago in August 2005,) or the other one full name; perhaps even "larking" book and movie title with details same name starring actress which is *Fault in my Stars*. Not infringement by me here in this chapter, I'm hazy in this pressurized re-memory. These were professionally similar to conquests in the social problems and caring fields in my elections participation/career, in consideration of this about the projects along time for kismet maybe. Special Delivery for something we talked about if I not intercepted but I did facebook.com to her about credit to one short auto response I dug but couldn't make out the meaning. Read below more. I need more than a sign, strength emotionally time building an. No mean cease and desist, these stars are more fraud than I ever will be like most singles. )

(These stars' online media solved a problem in recognition I have previously mentioned in VGG a little enough as far as I know. I look into social problems and my school board goal was about interpersonal interaction stronger. Made permissible by my every-where advocacy or legal writing as the ED goal on the document see last chapter of this work, or with Looky Lou's next to me on that very Board. Or some dinner table make believe that I would take for scouting for my wife material subjects for movie maker prowess as much as movies made in 90s I have yet to claim. I'm "rosey" in spirit for my perspective and success outlook, it's just damn ugly for me that some people to steal each and every shred of verbal output that I said or did or wrote places from me that should be my nude credits worth something and money too to me.)

(My environment is one-source piracy much of me, using Gregg K. Jann as target and source perspective designer to no credit to Gregg K. Jann or the money goes not to him. I am not homeless, own a nice KIA Soul, and have legal standing and set up help, and a trademark in which these credits and money may have wiggle room to not just drop Social Security I have.)

(Hollywood can cram money for my claimed projects and MHSA not just Sacramento, CA to get the nude credits working right legal with my name in the industries my IP has entered once recognized as mine by you. I wrote you on Facebook.com 2 pictures and you are different. However, I did tell someone Shailene a month before A Jann Plan was published I was first and original with AIDS name and acronym and wanted a date to Pulitzer Awards to set up you for goodness too. Did I help with Adrift, because the writer won that award some year? I am a much older man, and coincide with you personally in activist not as much energy me. I'm a Who's Who ethical man as I write you each of the times, a former elected, accomplished, but don't get a recommendation in a black out/ban cover up by a bad men and lady stealing. I am getting this corrected in these my first four books, also known as Gregg K. Jann *Epic Tomes IV Ply*.)

## Continuing with Feeling

I should win a medal worth money for designing a tax act in California for Health care while occupationally on my own related to counseling paid work getting punished chemically for it and hurt in ways for being too moral and too good. Prizes awarded I want for Gregg Kevin Jann–not nominated by self just shows you where to look for authenticity and credit of the deserving accomplishment:  MEDICINE for schizophrenia recovery consumer design (my Inherent value source perspective design medicine for nice legal guy) not just my own cooperation but my contributions in IP efforts and my youth/adult managed care invention (Santa Rosa/Sonoma Co. Medical Association ED N. A. B's pool yard original to me, funding prop 63)and first and original disease names with my survival; nonfiction LITERATURE in getting the legal word out for- "clergymen blindness", teach peace, and authentic economy and book design particularly *Van Goghing Gregg*; ECONOMICS for nude and source perspective designer credits and Safety Net Economy theory, union MH consumer work rights, even internet role if ever proven; PEACE for winning the Cold War without participating in negotiation or known bully ostensibly, and religious/school adding in kindness certain sect.; CHEMISTRY for Social Responsibility instruction and changes emanating; PHYSICS for US not knowing Gregg in unrequited manner to him for all Gregg K. Jann has done and the fame of my word smiths and other stolen credits.

I cannot nominate myself in highly prestigious awards in a note to all who are readers, I just told you where to look and confirm and verify and send to a high cabinet government official or previous winner or University professor authorized to do so for me who is Gregg Kevin Jann(remember I write nonfiction and am a cover up by business and government: point being I want out of false imprisonment for I never committed a crime I was not authorized righteous to do by my Lord and Savior to get the word out as an active Conscientious Objector reserving government elections/income and property rights/and spouse and family which were discriminated brought to my attention, which I did not pursue legal action but the discrimination lawyer who told me did do just that – discriminated me from having a girlfriend.

You know the type of man those attorneys are, and honest is not one of their qualities about them but they can look up in respect Gregg K. Jann for not wanting to sue if at all possible. The only thing a doctor knows is hire a prostitute in gym clothes for someone needing humanizing and wanting a female relationship to his inexperienced man known to try to be in the movies and he was elected like he told the law.

I was smart enough a US Commended Student graduating high school, starting in the National Merit program 1st grade, maybe scrambled in the brain soon, and hurt sometime definitely college freshmen year for being an unknown hero while a teen running for US President like I was one (see prior publishing). It could have been the crowd of high students thought I was "gay" and I wasn't ever teased about it, who knows for I said, "be a priest" in a minister's family business not your own. It is wrongful to also call someone else "un-so and so" for wanting peace around Israel as I observed happened. I am an advocate, bare bones, and did work on the most value on Earth while injured now more recovery.

I deny nations primarily in strategy, groups of people, and regimented social compliance their own heroes for I am a better man. Both name-calling "gay" and "un-so and so" from people who aren't as idealistic, make less text book style history, and I use them well so I know where the redneck is for money to collect is. I said "gay" like you weren't a strong football player in junior high school, and always knew it didn't matter except I wanted to play on a winner. Maybe somebody drugged the varsity team to get smaller, and my former teeth were an example khaki in color now capped white not shown much to the eye even in my digital photos or bathroom mirror.

Of course, I can't afford an always recognized graduate degree except I was a grad student in Economics having earned a 2nd-BA from Sonoma State University. I always shared my own output and ability in all 3 colleges I graduated, some monkey thinking that I was verbally loved as a peer educator in classes and newspaper helping to be included in Marquis Who's Who in America, Health Services Section. Maybe to N. Committee; mark my occupation as Screen Writer to bust them up in Hollywood, those film and television credits were stolen and I want them, I without knowing who stole them in the first place.

At present if Lawyer, I'm too poor for my own family, and don't own a home and want them. I own a late enough model car and if you just want to take me for a spin for those young women out there– I think you have to usually pay Dutch or all of it as I'm on Social Security income early and can earn my way off from proper financial crediting recovery to my person held/forwarded/protected by JannDA.com myself. I have been off all disabled supports from working in past and owe nothing legally still. I am not strange except I scream in punishment for Christ Like words occasionally for religious persecution. I contributed the most of any MH consumer to the fields and professions. Don't you see what a business degree from Chico State University can do by my own word and reckoning in above note for Awards I want to win truthfully in merit if so and with my previous publishing and during my elections.

A normal man has family and home, and it is what I want for my talent but who stole my credit? I want it back and with the money I should be valued at. Don't you think de-Pirating Western Economy and charging Russia for techniques to be honest and caring with pay for true to origin people according to Gregg K. Jann would help. USA to earn money righteously and inclusively to make our social economy fair; with respect making authentic dignity and sources richer and all more honest in a changed system. - An Econ degree thesis conceptualizations and words together not taught to author ever anywhere, in Business schools or newspapers or prior or outside activity.

Now about nude credits and source perspective design needing to be accurate for work done and already attributed albeit not ever recognized Truth to Origins. I sang and acted a one man play of "It's a Long Way to Tipperary" about a 100 years ago war between Ireland and England, like they had when I did it when I was a child circa 60s to 70s.. The play was set between Great Britain and Irish Republican Army I heard now settled since a

while ago. At least I did the performance before a young astron-
omy brother not known if he knew I was a Person to remember
his upbringing with joy, if not however strangely possible I could
have verbally created this original screen play and then completely written and performed this play. I viewed the same play I
performed except with many actors to fill in my performance
zone writing while in these recent past few months in front of my
television since last book Van Goghing Gregg I authored. The
play I acted was on TV Public Television station channel 9 from
San Franciso near my home town of Santa Rosa, of the North
Bay Fires fame. The play could have been reading to me while I
was in a mind zone very young to entertain my brother, or I am
a play write who performed worth nude credits once recovered
whole. I don't do this type of performance in front of people in
private life usually when its overwhelmed and so strange to my
upbringing, but over a long haul of familiarity I know many mental health endeavors are mine with special needs thingy to inherit
family ownership and sister care and hopefully I have a place to
put educated MIS endeavors, all else when I am broken, and my
words are true and unique chosen by God and Man through him,
which is me Gregg K. Jann.

A rarity from me and my shyness to even perform the play
alone in audience of one when I was that young if not inanimately
programmed by friends to me and mother Medical Association
family, and also suspicion how could the VIPs reach modern era
television as the credits of screenwriting this about Irish play were
another person that could be accurate of printer and written de-
scriptions of set and more actors in what to do along the lines of
my Book of the Play Act. Looking up Tipperary of some type
online, the encyclopedias only report that the play and songs is

accurately Irish but documented about World War I fighting alongside England even saluted later by Soviet Red Army singing.

Censors, no child labor, force feeding burning my virgin ears programming me unknown could be revisionist history of a play I wrote or just remembered I performed are factors of fudging. Critical thinking, writing, putting on performance for color enhancement and relate ability can be quite stimulating and downright shaking to make a kinder establishment with tolerance to treason for reasons of kindness or love and religious acceptance of non-violence and for greater rules of freedom, love, and peace justice if we are careful not to upset dangerously but let rabble rousing occur to change us and empower other them to us for betterment. Or just entertainment of course and de-program the mind of a creator. Or just some college student stole a hand me down script and made himself a name on Public TV.

I meant by surprise performance to have a reality show for later outer space for my brother to be an astronaut like he was capable of, instead of dangerous research of cause and effect of inner space mental illness unlike my potential research project of correlation studies of disease and parents occupation left at Delta Dental of California when I was an temporary employee with title of Assistant Actuarial Analyst straight out of college working in a place I wanted to work of San Francisco, CA.

You wrote a **review** for *your most often Restaurant* in Santa Rosa, CA not far on foot

Yesterday


11/3/2017

Good food, and exceptionally quick service while I eat alone. I cannot afford two. I gave this establishment a review to them a waitress and explaining a pseudonym that is mine of "August Tip", and the staff or owner seemed to get me recognized on Prabook.com. Now about specifics…. I'll skip to things about Gregg, me.

November 2017

**Things I Love**

Innocence, morals, good people if you can find them and introduce them to me like I teach, opportunities, public service, recognition; co-aligned goals of kindness, authenticity, and making it in economy money wise; and good pussy in pretty women

**Find Me In**

Sonoma County, Church, Bible Study, Santa Rosa Democratic Club

**My Blog Or Website**

*jannda.com*

**When I'm Not Doing Eating**

I reflect from lifetime taking in trainings/past education, walking, sports on TV, news, occasional daytime talk show favorite host Kelly, format The View next

**Why You Should Read My Reviews**

When I do it on *jannda.com*, it's with a health services business tax license

**My Second Favorite Website**

*wikipedia.com*, or etymology dictionary because I made up words all my life

**The Last Great Book I Read**

*Van Goghing Gregg* by Gregg K. Jann, and a fish oil book on clearance

**My First Concert**

Elton John at Berkeley Community Theater with a friend in 1982

**My Favorite Movie**

The Good, The Bad, and The Ugly from my Channel 2 viewing teen days

**My Last Meal On Earth**

steak

**Don't Tell Anyone Else But...**

I'm lactose intolerant and know an MD hurt me to have it for peer counseling business

**Most Recent Discovery**

I think words spoken origins are credited like bar room fights, mine ahead WWI

**Current Crush**

Shailene Woodley because I thought she was not raunchy. I paid a price liking her telling a Professional in her office in my friendly manner I could meet her by writing a screen play explaining I write. The dentist prescribed some biological damage.

**On Good Reads. Com currently written by author**
**Excerpt and additional text and below paper work email style**
**for Autobiography and Book Design Awards applications**

## Questions About Van Goghing Gregg: Recovery Toward Love By Gregg K Jann

Reader Q&A
**Safety Net Economy**
"Unanswered Questions (1) by author Gregg K. Jann, who talked originally about this below form of caring economy at Chico State University while studying and working on MIS in mid 1980s as a student trying to invent the internet by creating Peace Themes (building from A Jann Plan, specifically in Bettering the World – both are Good Reads.) – Gregg Jann insert"

What do you think about Gregg K. Jann's ideas about a nude economy with new credits to be recognized truthfully throughout the country? Parts and starts anywhere in the process need given credit for the truth to origin, even if later like in a contract hold or trust. Which is an authentic economy vis-à-vis capitalism and its piracy of the origins. Safety Net Economy discriminates as Gregg spoke hurt in CSU Chico.

"Answer personally: Gregg K. Jann was discriminated in knightly battle, from "murder on the Orient Express" while too young before CO status enough solidified, in running for US President in a declared statement nothing else, to caring about old people as a test subject unaware to him, to being different due to week of his choice Vine Deloria book theme report in American History class at SRJC.-Gregg Jann insert

Verbal copy right documentation hard coded presently of **Safety Net Economy.** *V.C.R.@Gregg* Jann heard at California state work during Gregg Jann design of the Prop 63 Mental health services act before this passed election in 2004.

I said "Safety Net Economy" to my UC Berkeley-bound brother Scott when I was very young and I think him before college. Maybe People First starting with this concept phrase to give my credit to their favorite US President of America many philosophical things I said or did. I don't like it. I don't believe Roosevelt said Safety Net Economy in full or part as some in the Santa Rosa Democratic Club would have it to false origin, and I said Safety Net Economy more explanation Fifth Floor Whitney Hall 1982 Chico State University to a man who said, he was "Johnson." That his confusing name or that of the Great Society President's name was all he said, and I never saw him again as he did not live on the same dorms or floor I was on.

I was being robbed of speeches by people and attributed to Reagan, and I didn't like it. I did ask a few closed doors in a crazy wall no insight if people inside to get Great Britain to help me with no treason by me and unknown if credit reaches ever. Strange as I was a fan of Lady Diana for her virginity but what does a speech maker ban type of situation-o try to prevent when he was studying the internet before it was invented, adding up to too much stolen from someone. Gregg Jann added his own peace themes meant for the internet and our lives, outspoken in class about where to put money as community building meaning and peace connections with his legal case if ever needed for conscientious objector to all war on religious grounds which he spruced up with an anti-draft editorial at SRJC 1982(see Bettering the World, "Left page 1".)

What I say here is Safety Net Economy should not be a loan, and we should not punish but rather forgive and not falsely imprison people on supports like constricting disabled from heart to love or too poor from able to work out of social systems. Or not to truly put them in Debtors prison if charity offered to them can't be paid back. Upward Social Mobility can be done in ways; from MH recovery, to nicer HUD rooms, to well nice paying jobs and inheritances. Government Aid is an entitlement. Family and relatives need more than politeness, from receivers and truly needy need to try to earn love because that is what this is to the recipient. R. can do washing dishes and keeping the house clean and looking for work. Struggles and minor conflicts of not getting along need forgiveness, toleration, and acceptance which church teaches to not hurt each other too much or go over the line objectionable.

Nonprofits are a business and need the government and community to give them money, to pay salary and operate. A standard deduction is offered to ratepayers of taxes and more than covers for itemized deductions of most people yet we when in the nonprofit sectors need money and other donations like volunteer labor sometimes. Churches do too, and need gratefulness like all the SN Economy participants and providers to be human.

In a large scale, a government like a Third World Country could run a Safety Net Economy and be better than communism, with more freedom and care. Revenue from the driving engines of production paying taxes to those at the bottom rungs needing support, and we all need care and support no matter what walk of life we are especially at the end.

Did someone steal me, in taking Safety Net Economy without me being first to the copy right office? I was discriminated after business and economics classes and hurt in resumes send outs looking for professional computer work after each of my 2 bachelor degrees. I had a lifetime of low salary. I always cared about people, and wanted a female beautiful wife with class and morals. Do I get one now that I called you on it – here in this text and mention of 1st definition by Jann in Book III by Gregg K. Jann.

Category: Biography/autobiography
Title: Van Goghing Gregg: Recovery Toward Love
Publisher: Rose Dog Books/Dorrance Publishing
Author: Gregg K. Jann
Editor: Self Gregg K. Jann

Description: Right off the bat in *Van Goghing Gregg* by Gregg K. Jann we read ultimate self-defense details against murder conspiracy cult in first person. Later we see a vignette with more insight for engagement safety in bear wrestling. These two incidents happened in Gregg's teen years, outside his awareness lasting 35 years. Nonfiction accounts make *Van Goghing Gregg* a recovery book to him, now stronger 3rd pass periscopic inside looking deeper in publishing Mr.Jann's 2 previous poly sci books on mental health. VGG provides philosophy movements and themes Gregg may have created while too young, and is more than adventure of a Nor Cal silent legend, which in explanation he was both blurting out expressions and making history both wherever he went. Gregg K. Jann's self-styled nude credits invention he copy wrote are like a piece of furniture, hand crafted with him more congealed than a crazy designer he may have been but stolen. Revealing sources grown immense in economy and ledger domain, USA appears unable to recognize truth to origins in our creativity except for Mr. Jann 3 books including *Bettering the World* and *A Jann Plan*. Gregg Jann's career uncovers aspects of chemical imbalance and harm to abstinence proponents and church reformers in speculation, and we see Gregg's career of source perspective designer role advocates ownership of creativity and IP reform in teaching peace through Character Ed as a former school board member in Santa Rosa at Piner-Olivet USD near the current fires, and author may have had a community safety role in stopping the fires by policy at district boundary. Gregg K. Jann's was kind as a counselor and educator/writer assisting mental health consumers starring also as a public official and union negotiator in the Mental Health Field. Gregg K. Jann throughout this writing uses examples like a profession in that he knows about the piracy of consumers, and The American citizen Jann is and as The Honorable Gregg Jann serves others in treatment, law, and de-stigma here in *Van Goghing Gregg* and in his life. We need to know a hero, particularly with the North Bay fires going on currently with their aftermath at application date, and Mr. Jann designed the Mental Health Services Act to get into Marquis Who's Who in America for his accomplishments many and un-ethically attainted. Gregg Jann is legal himself and law abiding, never in jail and not ever an inmate of any type, and is legally contributory.

Applicant for Book Contest Name: Gregg K. Jann

From Jann Demystifying Affects Products Page on Jannda.com with a health business tax license:

Book Published June 2017 is *Van Goghing Gregg: Recovery Toward Love*

*Van Goghing Gregg* shows more a philosopher in stopping a murder spree cult in San Francisco's Marin Headlands area.

Cover depicts respect for medical divinity and processing needed by the community. VGG reveals Gregg doing in his background that is insightful to Mr. Jann being a great source perspective designer of history since the 70s. Buy from online booksellers or Rose Dog Books directly under nonfiction autobiography/memoirs.

Hint: Like Tsars might be sick to them that had them in leadership, I think fathers should call their daughters Princess especially if extra needed or deserved. I read and assess Russia called too many people some type of title in the 1800s fiction literature. Our community of Sonoma County may be kinder to one economy magnet of the disabled, in a way to be gentle to the figurative folk or my Old Lady. I'm embarrassed by my writing, and I never was educated in college to write English composition as I rushed through cut short on time based on my ability to do expression. I played hurt while young for 2 decades and completed all requirements of colleges for degrees in three colleges, 2 bachelors distinct from each other in time and place - one a graduate school operation.

Online Review for National Outlet: not shown and not published in many drafts

Down the Street Book Store in Former Retail Space of Same Name of Apartment

*Van Goghing Gregg* is an outstanding non-fiction philosophy book from some action hero when a California North Bay teenager. The biographical themes in this book goes against a mass murderer cult conspiracy Chapter One. It is written in easy words in Jann's plain style, who went on to get a Business Administration degree from Chico State. VGG starts exciting as a thriller and mystery to solve a crime as it is occurring. (Crime happened mostly in the 1970s.) Keep reading the book past the

Chapter One details to find out more characterizations and greater themes to an innocence truncating an adulthood. We read in the Bible about the fabled Mustard Trees growing from the smallest seed, and we know from the 60s about Flower Power, both of which may have roots from the young author's Jesus vision as documented in *Van Goghing Gregg*. *Van Goghing Gregg* overall portrays a beautiful young person, and if his Environment today wonders an affliction against his will to hurt for some unknown reason as he produces care or de-stigma occupationally. The philosophy of "why me' is not explored about chemical imbalance and Consumerism, but rather we read a recovery from someone owning a health license and mental health trademark in his sole proprietorship writing philosophy of the era, which may have been started by Jann himself. *Van Goghing Gregg* is a quick read, has emotion and feelings well done, and it's good to study for origins. Gregg K. Jann and his 3 books and ongoing blog contains ideas we need in industry, government, law, and mental health in kind story forms making interesting format.

Signed: Presidents' August Tip

Doctor Professor of Most Classes at Chico; LinkedIn Message: Do you know me at all?
Sep 1, 2017
Congratulations on another good, longstanding work milestone!! Finished writing my philosophical memoir of the underpinnings of my source perspective designer role of most history making unrecognized since and before Chico State era with US President Reagan speech making. Read my cover, for you may remember me as an outspoken student and I alluded to running for president and asking for help in forwarding my sister's word to you of

"blog" saying it's what I do -I was a printed political commentary in college newspapers 3 of them. Sister said that word askance once at hacienda house about when I said I wanted to be a priest to be different than my dad, like I was in first grade and it wasn't my religion or any real to me and later I used it as license to re-form due to punishment.

See how remarkable I am to remember something like that, and knowing she was having real fun in copying my ability in word make up and that she didn't know what it meant. It was a long time ago, when I told you to no reminder and I know this meeting was a long time for you to remember. It must help a lot in my source perspective designer credits true, now the money comes or. Is it because I'm not Catholic, or people blanked me stolen by Reagan speech writer who did say stole me on campus, or you think the next sentence and the next one after that is not a hero worth your time, money, and a life worthy. Were you drugged to forget the greatest man you ever met, as what happens to teacher? *Van Goghing Gregg: Recovery Toward Love* at Rose Dog Books online bookstore under autobiography in nonfiction where I stopped a murder cult of Marin County in Chapter One con-tinuing from A Jann Plan. Exciting, easy to read, and it shows my public posted blog abridged of the Safety Net economy to counter communism in social services where I am at in Santa Rosa still as a hot bed of political activity. I designed the MHSA with notice in Marquis Who's Who in America, Health Services Section, but to no money from the governor or county for my RFPs or grants to me yet. A little money recognition and I would be more serious than my letter to you and some others asking for School of Business Alumni of the Year. 12:22

**Electronic Series continued with Notes to Her:**

I told people I didn't want to rape my childhood, by writing over-the-line personal stories or giving too much information. It goes to adulthood and present. I may have, and intended some info for a lawyer. I walked into an esquire office a potential local HQ about a pressing lawsuit to open I have not shown concern about but a good lawyer needs to know I was hurt. I just met one from Democratic politics, and he was at a picnic ostensibly a fundraiser started during my time on the Sonoma County Democratic Central Committee in the 90s. I over ate to break the bank.

It looked like he was shot by Hernandez for Piner-Olivet or the County Schools, after the jump suit wearing attorney said he was looking for a case in his slowing down days and he was going the next day to San Francisco court to file something so, "he would not talk to media." It was weird to look at the whole scene, not just what he wore, and the eyes of a guest look like a devil worshipper. I kissed a woman name game that I thought I knew and she was drop dead gorgeous and later seemed about 15 years old except the woman she chose to replicate image was a college grad about 26. She was sitting, got up when I walked by, straight armed me stiffly elbow crooked when I tried to kiss her once because I paid her from personal funds not to be a prostitute as a farewell to DC in 2012, I followed through 2nd time and she let me smack her on the lips, and I felt a falling leaf on my front as we kissed-probably some kind of hand job outside my shirt with my penis sticking out of my pants turned on.

I enjoyed The Real Woman and the real memory of the campaign worker I knew in Obama's re-election of 2012, because I heard about "a marriage or nothing kind of guy". I feel used without knowing and spent ragged and keep trying for a wise moral inner and outer beauty to save my reputation. The mental hospital administrator at the picnic offered me her hot dog with relish on it, and we talked that she disagreed with me that the SMART rail was not a toy train. I said it was, without telling her I saw light people at the Civic Center bus stop in attempted murder for my great fleece coat. I don't think train and bus get along, and I think our train is a hoax for I not hearing it often and not seeing steps boarding it at stations. It's great to have, and I wish the train was to be.

I believe in local taxes for my support of great projects unsupported by federals and state government enough, and also for example I may have started the whole craze. In 90s I designed a poster with Bob Tunks committee head of Guns to Toys for parents not to give toy guns to their children over Christmas like at Kmart. I forgot who the illustrator was, she did a great job as I suggested a train and she morphed it from a tank. I have stories of my Grandfather August Jann being a rail road engineer/station master in Wisconsin, being the family bread winner for my G.M., my father Donn and our murdered uncle Burleigh from WWII who was a sharp shooter in Normandy. I believe movie *Saving Private Ryan* used and mispronounced "Jann" in filming a same character realist spoken by the star in France on set.

As I was talking to the 3 including the young woman about the Nobel winner from Pakistan on my blog in August when this fundraiser picnic happened,  All but the girl dove below the table with color bands of light blocking the site below them. I couldn't see past the band of color, and left the party solo taking a long walk around.

This lawyer might oppose me, or he might be very good. A good lawyer with a lot of time on his calendar is useful to me, except I don't know if something happened to him as Facebook.com looked like he's taking on a big case for causing fire, death, and destruction recently. I'm in limbo, and didn't get past the secretary of his office as the law I want money for is secret or confidential, and threatening to me. Keep publishing, because we have to stop the intentional problem of maiming and disabling for difference of opinion saying occupational hazard some.

To: Non-profit work Supervisor

12/18/17 response:  keep me posted about jury duty

Thanks and I will be at the company Christmas party.

Also, I have Jury Duty starting to show up or call January 15th. Not necessarily picked, and some time before special work gig at the University. I want to work regular gig, but I think I waited too long to cancel jury duty as I had 5 days about 1 1/2 weeks ago.

I want Jury Duty as I never get called (it's been 2 decades), and I think my legal status and un-Pirating economy advocacy might be helped in speculating if I go - selected or not without a medical excuse to get out of it.

Gregg Jann

## Is This Sales Memo Why I Was Called into Jury Duty? Or was it the girl at above end?

San Francisco Book Store Owner

[December 13, 2017 after a good 2 days/nights celebrating Xmas Tree Lights at Union Square, Cable Car rides in the Sun, and San Francisco's Fisherman's Wharf, Pier 39, and walking down Market Street]

Please carry for your book store shelves to sell local author Gregg K. Jann's non-fiction books. He is an educated Marquis Who's Who in American former elected official.

*Van Goghing Gregg* (June, 2017)- Autobiography/Mental health philosophy- Rosedog Books author Gregg K. Jann

*A Jann Plan* (Dec 2014) - political science/commentary /"teach peace education law suggestion", Rosedog Books author Gregg K. Jann

*Bettering the World* - Red Lead Press of Dorrance, Gregg K. Jann ends the draft and reduces threat of Cold War and begins Abstinence Education, include campaign literature of a professional leading changes, and a sales paper with non-violence in schools

Gregg K. Jann is Marquis Who's Who in America designer of legislation, a resident of Santa Rosa, CA and a former elected school board member. In *Van Goghing Gregg: Recovery Toward Love* (June 12, 2017; Rose Dog Books, Pittsburg, PA) , author Gregg recounts his high school encounter with the Trail Side Strangler and gay accomplices in Pt. Reyes while back packing with friends over Easter Break sophomore year. Chapter 1 defense of gruesome details "on the seashore bluff" made a hairy re-memory process spread over this VGG book and in *A Jann Plan* (Dec 1, 2014; Rose Dog Books, in which Gregg K. Jann also documents he named AIDS originally and had a role inventing the internet, as well founded the Mental Health Services Act - CA Prop 63 in 2004).

Gregg K. Jann is significant in accomplishment although not given credit like a stolen speech writer, is a local figure since kindergarten and lived in Marin working retail management after studies at Chico State University, and this book shows a philosopher stopping a religious cult of mass murder by vigilante justice and bravery. Gregg Jann was never in a trial, but should he be a plaintiff for more significance to regain vastly used intellectual property nationalized or stolen by piracy of a MH consumer and political speechmaker?

Author believes in freedom of speech, and that in Gregg K. Jann can recover when we know him and his bravery that he was in a haze for 35 years forgetting. *Van Goghing Gregg* is Gregg K. Jann's 3rd non-fiction book, and he's been appointed, elected, and worked as an employee in the mental health field for 20 years including increasing union labor rights to a disenfranchised work force. Currently he is a presenter for a non-profit and a sole proprietor.

November 30, 2017

Gregg Jann, a NAMI member and In Our Own Voice Presenter from our Sonoma County affiliate, has published his third non-fiction book. His most recent is titled *Van Goghing Gregg: Recovery Toward Love* (Rose Dog Books) and is categorized autobiography/memoirs and is lightly worded on philosophy that he spoke while too young. He may have been original and may get the credit in these words, which his 2nd book A Jann Plan (shortened title) contains mental health essays and other essays and a law suggestion to un-Pirate Western Economy for a greater peace.

Gregg wonders if he was hurt by criminology without author present in a trial at end of book, without much ado of a "why me" manner about his alleged incident with San Francisco's Trail Side Strangler with a group of men in Pt. Reyes National Seashore when he was back packing with his family and friends. Ironic that he helped to stop a cult murder spree, to no word from the sheriff or witnesses, as the author was in a haze and forgot his details for over 35 years. His recovery process includes re-memory in therapy, and he has largely regained details he never held in his short-term memory.

Gregg Jann writes mainly political science books with philosophy embedded for his originality and economics end point he says he is, with nude credits he copy wrote. The other legendary incident Gregg Jann covers over both *A Jann Plan* and *Van Goghing Gregg* as he remembered more and more of his teenage years was a bear wrestling fight in Banff, BC.

On other notes, Gregg Jann was an elected official in education in Santa Rosa, CA while a survivor/ MH consumer, and survived a New York subway runaway in the mid-1980s while he was visiting his father who worked across Columbia University on Broadway.

## Sometimes it's Good Not to Consult
Submitted on Fri, 2017-11-17 14:46

Under the category of too much information, or do it yourself movement, or beware of scammers; we need to use discernment and sometimes not listen like we are told to people who use persuasion sell.

The worst idea jiggered up in my mind was wrong or not di-agnosis by professionals in using Trauma Care, not specific mental illness like schizophrenia in the DSM IV like I was taught in college while working in the field, now DSM V. TC seemed to chart a complete sheet of effects all sides of feelings, reactions stated to LCSW completely not reaching recovery and not therapeutic trust.

*Prevention and Health*

## World AIDS Day December 1st each Year

Submitted on Sat, 2017-12-02 14:47

Today marks World AIDS Day, started by 2 men both UN in Switzerland in 1988. One was a former San Francisco TV journalist named Bunn. I feel I named AIDS originally while transferring into Chico State University '82. I have told my story here at Jannda.com and in 2 books.

Don't mind if right information on genesis. A shy man means no harm when I worked Sr. Assistant Manager in Woolworths in the City. Volunteering at Face to Face before employed counselor at the mentally ill group home was good learn to care more than acknowledgement.

*Property Rights and Ethics*

## Each Person Matters - from Bible Study

Submitted on Thu, 2017-12-14 15:49

It's a kind management professor, not in Psychology that doesn't, that teaches each person matters. We met over Proverbs Bible Study. He hoped he taught classes not to resent people. My college peers had "no talk rules" like No Credit policies from on up high. I was nicer and more thoughtful, of itself discriminated by money and Big City.

Calling my college Chico Normal School by some lead my understanding to not reveal SMI to prevent sabotage of mind and health by others. Connection makes peers wiser - what we want if possible.

*Holistic Community and Permaculture*

Publisher Editor Services:

*Truth to Origin from an Elected Survivor* or *Epic Tomes IV* by Gregg K. Jann is at the US copyright.gov office under process submitted November 13, 2017. We could together get the book published and get the word out of what I think the world is doing for nuclear engagement of a Reagan speaker and peacenik American. I'm an injustice in health and money – do foreign countries know me and do they know I said as source in administration 'tear down this wall," as Real Ronnie speaker if such were to be true recognized. For me to assert with certainty standing forth at a future conjecture of time with me as one man and the time as geopolitical wanting more end to war and more answer for peace both in Europe and around the world.

I added I heard in a drugged, sleepy haze (like I invented the legal status of "forced technical virgin" of having unknown sex like white fright or something hurt in the military), that someone warned my town screaming, "Geronimo" the night of a TV reported fire strike. Looking at an 8 mile cross section of town, it was flattened and blackened more like a fire bomb or H bomb destroying 24,000 homeless or casualties - I'm not classified to know for sure but I am surrounded by people who are and my book describes my thought process of brainstorming creativity to come up with answers I know from past and in my head.

The book says the guilty of piracy of early internet inventiveness of Gregg K. Jann was religious war. The proposed answer can be called in the classroom as "Teach Peace + 2", as the book's is titled more like "Truth to Origin" as the Amendment for US Constitution if ever get that far no matter who the president or congress is in defining, providing legal re-definitions, and altering text if need be. I can get more political and in political circles at the Democratic Club selling drink tickets, as one former president here in town.  I have a voice, and can't work so hard due to disability which gives me the right and privilege to understand the needs for paragraph 2, and the victim's restitution paragraph 3 is an angle for my consumer credits stolen a lot in my 3 so far published books.

This one book of Truth to Origins is that of a muckraker, known now that one religion stole from me at Chico and Santa Rosa/to Seattle on internet in the mid '80s, even discriminated at work including San Francisco.  Don't be turned off from publishing if I tag a religion that may be yours.  I advocate for Reconciling Methodist, but they don't mentor me like my father's Presbyterian seems to in my bible study group now that I'm in my middle 50s.

If North Bay October fires were a bomb in Santa Rosa starting war, the guilty is those stealing IP and making author worthless monetary and hurt while in poor health treatment.  I did not charge unnecessary in book Truth to Origin from former Elected Survivor, ensuring MH consumer Gregg Jann and his family from his parents meaning brothers and sisters, their/my spouses and children and the in laws all are innocent, mainly for Gregg's non-violence answers with criminal justice legal contributory in IP elsewhere too.

The IP theft is not just business, as the state of California took Gregg Jann's design of Prop 63 in 2004 and poisoned him instead of remunerating him justly as he wants the state to do with liability payments to Gregg for harm done in their state's and state employee's denial and delay. Gregg K. Jann designed the Mental Health Services Act, providing the funding tax source, and the MH consumer perspective in meetings in Sacramento early in process that kept with ballot initiative design: I was working part time, and then full time as a counselor appointed on union negotiations and California Network of Mental Health Clients where all I did my own design work on my self-initiative.

## Inundated with Body Doubles Bad if Just One Pretty Lady as Acting Troupe Needing Recovery

## Prevention and Health

## Not submitted but here to health business license dot.com at Jannda.com

## An Effort for Strangeness in Confusion then to Stability Heal for someone we need: or is it to discount and disqualify someone?

Not noticing whom your wife is, or not taking the time to take a break from the busy body you are is damnation. Forced into a mold, from a glass wall that a person can't get out and feel the warmth needed from a partner is wrongful. With a Cap Grass problem and no explanation from Social Security examiner in this diagnosis, just knowledge that family filled out the forms and has a conflict of interest in keeping you under wraps, tied down, and not exploring the world of business like you studied and claim to have produced in competition with their adopted home state of Washington is a disclaimer.

My family is not bad to me to provide a rock and staying my social life, because diagnosis includes delusional, but I am cleared up of that problem and cured. I have no grandiosity of mania, also cured before stated by me to doctor to begin re-memory processing. I am just blocked, and need freedom in America. These are my writing non-fiction 4 books, in poly sci. with my philosophy enhancements for USA, with examples I know of IP stolen and providing wisdom in the field of mental health in that I have not ever been incarcerated or an inmate of any kind and am legally contributory denied by corruption and money to legal authority liars. I'm the wholesome spirit, creative with Holiness on mind and heart, and moral to the bone. Yes, I was attacked, but those are what you get when you are a Moral Teacher in the USA including Abstinence Teacher in the editorial pages of several local newspapers for the young, the mentally disabled, and for my wife hunt.

I must seem crazy to never have talked about my college exploits for no watered-down product of my mind, as family doesn't believe in consumer empowerment. You should for civil rights to meet the rubber on the road in economy. I had to keep my adventure and achievement to myself, to defend against, and keep alive from attacks from US President to his men to Industrialists to churchmen. Maybe just calling for the end of Gregg K, Jann's sacrifice for his Sainthood or for anybody he wants to be in health, and beginning of commercial advancement to his own riches or just money like everybody he could now be like a powerful politician, to controlling shareholder of corps, to bank ownership, to a movie producer, to land owner big and small properties.

It's a nasty church that is replaced member by member, couple by family, even regular attendance can't keep up Mafia style replacement actors. Family holidays no less are violated by de rigueur actors replacing people like Russian counterparts to keep members happy from clinical depression. I informed police, my lawyer, mental health poison police, and all they say is that maybe these my family are wearing  make-up or tell me to enforce the trusts within family bonds by threatening my sanity like they always assumed I was crazy.  I am of sound mind, just can't work sustainably and low wages are oppressive to all my IP regain efforts, writing, and contacting the world wide of my past present future tense.

I diagnose I am catching on to noticing the similar looking people, and know the difference in my eyes and Capgrass Transference with no doctor to thank.  I study hard at my entertainment media, mainly my favorite actress Shailene Woodley.  I'm sorry I keep mentioning her, but it was damned not to know different people filling in same shoes in my life and this actresses' media helped me. My mom developed more warmth in me for my interpersonal use and carry within myself, where does diplomacy come?  Do pictures if I take them with a camera toward models and BDs make too big a difference to insanity threats, within poisoned mental health systems and informants roughed up and readier?

Maybe timid in dating women who are not moral and not bold to my presence 1st hand, but no liar am I.  Just mentoring socially and in business is needed, not coaching from law unless I need to be for a rich person I am deemed.  I'm not awkward ever in my life to my knowledge.  I never hurt someone other than ultimate self-defense.  I was lying low in living danger since Chico State University, and I prove it true as victim of IP theft greatly and in receiving bodily harm.  I am brave in fighting against corruption in drug mental health care, and at employment in paramilitary structures of the mind.  I added to treatment from the hurt and pain I was given, all perhaps to hide my candidate for the US President for elections. I was elected with standing for public scrutiny and putting forth non-violence for more than school children.

The Honorable Gregg Jann is as fair as a judge in not taking what is not his. Please pay him handsomely in large sums of money with a pretty woman too for meaningful relationships so he may be marital or married as he wanted.

# Chapter 5

### "Teach Peace +2"/*Truth to Origin*

Amendment
– Suggested US Constitution Amendment for Federal Jurisdictions and for the States to do our social/economic justices inclusive.

"For a kinder, gentler nation and to credit honestly sources for their economic ownership and civil rights, which together may prevent war home front to foreign struggles. This is justice to all Americans."
-Gregg K. Jann

The Jann Amendment
**Truth to Origin"**
**I. Teach Peace**
Encourage student learning opportunities in non-violence, social skills, character education, and general emotional well-being. Programs shall affect the entire campus culture, and shall include formal instruction in which students are required to participate. Staff will give progress reports to their local Governing Board four times each year.

## 2. Disabled; Elder; Each Persons Economic Rights

Any health, relationship, or disability status; or working in the advocacy profession or strong self-disclosure; or any status rated by public and private benefit organizations are ok for Author to receive book royalties for books sold anywhere. Same generally to consumer ownership rights for work performed, operated, or shareholder. Help accepted not required. Safety Net Economy existing, with debt forgiveness of public Entitlements. Recovery for persons with disability and quality to feel love is guideline for each. Living Salary/Wages to all job holders, owners, independent contractors; level according to Cost of Living for Region, subsidized.

## 3. Victim's Restitution

Creative Origins Advocacy deemed necessary to strengthen innovation authentic to any age sources ownership. Utilizing Social Responsibility to people out of your office and a gainful to (pot.) beneficiary form of Customer Service/Hold For Economy, we together determine victims' restitution payments for known crime, immediately or past statute of limitations if sum too large. Government pays if their own assignment is wrong, i.e. false origin; or if criminal too poor to make victim whole.

i.e. IP theft taken when unclear and not yet determined losses emanating for US and World Piracy, whether verbal and/or documented anytime source perspective designs and "larking" starts and parts of genesis endeavoring once proven by contributor with help if necessary.

## Source Perspective Designer = One Citizen: Gregg K. Jann /Jann Demystifying Affects™

The Jann Amendment brings us economic source perspective designer ability, suggested nude "larking" credits, and Government print up or transfer of money to an early internet "worker" drugged in the wrong professionals office when asking, 'where is Venture Capitalists" back home in Santa Rosa. This was recorded in his book II titled A Jann Plan on the very question of designing the internet with his own peace thesis to apply with his knowledge gained at Chico and cut for showing networking interest. This amendment works for banks, in ecology problems, stranger and ordinary crime elements, this list not all inclusive for what the people need for greater justice..

# Afterword

## Since "Eyoiu" Playing Socrates in NE

Playing both with child-like resolve and wisdom training in my Nebraska house circa 1965 age 3, I stated some of my philosophy tidbits original to me at least, to my mother over her chocolate upbringing teaching lessons and my toys accompanying as some words were previously reported and published in Van Goghing Gregg. My great "tear down this wall" speech heard decades later in Europe may have begun over my high wooden slat crib bed a few times originally to roust mother and father and brothers having "hardball" international intention meaning from me even then. I don't know who among father, mother, or the astronaut candidate brother in same room, any other family forwarded my speech to the President at the right time, combined with him saying it with the pounding fist same as I from when I first expressed it, for US President Reagan with our expensive missile expansion in Europe mid-1980s. When the Governor of the California state we were moving cross country to would profess his hard liner ways to Europe, I thought my brother would get a break into the space fellowship he needed. [Dad or brother didn't pay the political Candidate money for fundraising I don't believe and

I may have said to just a FAN who was student, so manned space flight is no morals particularly needing an un-Pirating Treaty/Law for USA in getting to and being in outer space, and for the Space Program to not disable competition in younger family members or community for "phee" h. D. money and education funds. We as one world should work down from orbital space in our Peace Treaties to enrich us and make better the common people of countries who live here. I said something like this as Reagan speaker and to same student family fundraiser who needed some help to graduate with a teacher's Masters to briefly hold a school job. I got laughed at by him alone in asking for a letter acknowledging from the Administration that I was an oral speech maker for US President Reagan that I wanted to help me get jobs and a better life. The request was done in the Hallway of the dorms at CSU, Chico. I think it was the famous speech writer who said, "I stole your credit" to me outside Kendall Hall of Chico State as I believed she traveled a distance one summer. She wrote books about the Reagans many years after '86 with a match according to photos.]

Looking back in accurate re-memory process, I took in my playfulness and thinking cap and said I was "Socrates" age 3 or 4 from father playing with me. It sounds funny like picking up clothes and laundry when saying this name aloud. It is funny to me, because my family was smart in some ways headed for colleges all 6 of the children for both parents were college graduates and as I graduated 2 different California State Universities. I read "book binding" around 14 years old, the process of re-making books even with old newsprint in the paper, perhaps yellowed chemically. With that other California State University, Long Beach not knowing much about who Socrates is, I get a sneaky suspicion sometimes over words and phrases very well known to me that are unfamiliar to science and when history is murky on the topic.

"Impetus" is a substitute for stolen "larking" energy spark of creativity, or even chores and errands and practical endeavors like technology – and I think saying "Socrates" after my Dad in a power struggle started mental illness from philosophy warnings in some or all Bibles not understood how Christianity grows ideology practices and our practical wisdom. I saved spending $170 on not replacing my vacuum cleaner, and prevented transferring the payment to personal Trust Administrator something like a $200 cleaning fee with the alleged report trouble associated that I could do it by accepting an "impetus" from her to "lark" my own energy creativity problem solving and acknowledging someone's threat and for me in myself to use a dull table knife low in the vacuum tubing where it meets the rollers to unclog it. LB State steals a lot of social rehab credit or just owns credit for this field. I don't know if CSU, Long Beach tries to take my writing and inventions as I don't work there and I am at Jann Demystifying AffectsTM or Jannda.com. I protect myself, my home, my IP, expand IP, and develop with combining civil and econ rights, and grow peace and Christian love and try prosperity for me and community some ways political with a mental health focus.

I am not just a minister's son, but something impressionable was said before 5 years old for all my life. It gave me Divine Right of a Philosopher/King (I'm former elected statesman, all rights reserved) to be born to my late father Reverend Donn G. Jann, and mother who said she was never like that. And businessman is what I work at in being for coinciding goals with humanity more Christian in trying for profit with tricky rules of government about money to moi, so I do non-profit Mental Health de-stigma Presenter for wages and travel reimbursement.

My father answered quietly to me solo, according to his Minister ideology to oppose philosophy when I stated I was "Socrates", that I was "King of Schizophrenia" age 4. He didn't berate or abuse me verbally over this. The words from him are probably from his and both parenting style, with a strong orator forceful disciplinary and a tough mother who was weaker. I was healthy pre-eighteen, never heard of the disease when dad said it too young perhaps for Space Program or for Military deferment rebuttal sacrificing someone too cute. One or many beautiful Minister's sons may be what it takes to cure the most dread mental illnesses, and I am not for it just if you read this warn these friends, that those of high social crime and grudge to the doctor's education and training. Most Mental Health consumers are expensive to treat with medicine and programs, and these consumer clients usually run afoul of the law and institutions. They take an understanding, and this understanding if we carry it suits well in foreign policy justices like France to name one country I sort of believe. We should have a treaty to not harm healthy people and not create new sick people to carry diseases that are man-made transfers of chemical, even in punishment especially if just parenting tastes in forceful behavior. We need Doctor's Law and Control that patients under research tests are limited intentionally to just one major disease if man-made or just not any more medically induced conditions if too suffering like mental illness—for Christian best care to one and to not harm.

Get a get a "C" in JC philosophy for saying Plato was Aristotle's student (when I think it might be Socrates who was teacher like my Dad and my CO main to chores), when I "reposited" T-Ball with a light ball on top of my head to my father's training on going to bat playing ball and I probably said such name standing with no plate below but I moving my arms. All American students can get a lift from credit given and proven to creative origins if built from a foundation taught making up their own work details. "Plato" meant not playing/teaching, maybe just opposite front man, or is/was counter to lead, or by asking questions, or we changed it to contributor even if mispronouncing the word "dinner" age 4. This is as I played to my Dad teaching smart stuff early age. Aside: I kind of believe Dana's around, for my in-denial case apart from blackout of news target marketing bans. I pray for no harm and not being hurt for person that sounded roughed up in media coverage, like real life or should I say "actual life" which I learned from feeling I am Titlist and wrote the Book of The 40 Year Old Virgin movie authored by an author Gregg K. Jann. I blame this and Outbreak movie IP theft from College, Law and Family types, Mental Health System, and San Francisco and Santa Rosa playing money Asshole with my career and earnings for their opportunity, blocking my political career in non-violence and writing, anything starring I suppose, even job hopefully not tourist or bus ride which I take in pedestrianly.

Re-memory is a wonderful process, startled by healthy mind just delivered to person and a jolt surprise force of mind working on a memory. The Chinese art character in A Jann Plan that looked like a picnic table with 2 eyes peering below got my bear wrestling together as best I could, thanks to the sales clerk too in that one healing with her cleavage, in person persona, and quiet time. The zits on my forehead later from med adjustment marked a coincidence with cure of grandiosity of mania or inaccuracies of delusions cold and got my mind to thinking back ward in success, and that I could win a legal case if needed. I never had the esteem that I could recover whole, and I wanted to piece elements and people of my information together to recollect my past story and where I have been in contributions to fields and professions even verbally once recognized by a business partner or legal team. I think of 2 persons in the movie Zero Dark Thirty for me in depictions among Arabs, both smiley to American good guys. One got hurt in a smallish cage to remember people, the other was a jovial guy cameo riding in a car for a photographer naturally to take his pic. (I'm white and American. German heritage with bloodlines all Great Britain nations and Irish surrounding Wales, which is excluded. Playing like a Prince Charles take-on could be as this heritage and bloodline info was from Dad verbally to me one sunny afternoon. My Grandfather on my mother's side said I was related to not 2 original US Constitution signers, at least one a double Founding Father on the Declaration of Independence. Good for religion here in America.)

This book's 9/11 Warning blog-style with the "M Therapy" could be Medicine using me intentionally to get poisoned for schizophrenia cure research, Military not liking what I do with no draft around just my legal draft registration with my supreme bravery at The Bluff with stories and my own ambition and my independent hopefulness for Advocacy on the Constitution(see Chapter 5); including religious staking territory for source perspective design of Reconciling Methodist for gay-others and COs, Mafia for punishment in social rehab unethically performed on author that weren't done on MH clients housed at Group Homes on conservatorship, or Mormons for lucky money and a convenient view of history first blush to draw them in or author swearing to sell books when he grew up never saying that "p" word slang for women sex organ, or those blocking Marriage for author by not making him any more competent in independence or judgement while he does fine as is except for high value money recognition.

I credit my schizophrenia recovery success besides pills and work to caring about the 60s, 70s, and 80s music scene in listening to rock radio from long ago in teen years, not just dancing with the prettiest women I could find. I had no lover but Christian accomplishment for Betterment of Mankind. The songs' romance themes were part I wanted and related to plus the rebellion I wanted to win since Make Love Not War simple youth interpretations held strongly in protest. The attention to me mostly in smiles at career position for responsible retail management work to get to the better prognosis in changing diagnosis to schizo-affective disorder to add mood mania. This stuff is what MH consumers need to know. My volunteer politics in the 90s just adding up as much as I could was the mania acknowledgement and filler, for healthy expression confided by retired Congresswoman Woolsey that she had relatable achievement zones. I kept a consistent tone in writing published to go with board roles in level steadiness. Caring in social responsibility to apply myself and then trying to earn money doing good things is turning the corner. I never got in trouble with the law, 'till trouble with a nurse who I didn't think was helping me Valentine's Day week 2018 in a crime investigation role not meant to heal.

This week a young teenage woman blinded me grey screen inside my eyes looking out while I was presenting in class in front of 4 other staff, 70 students, and had no recognizable feeling at the moment in me to what she reacted from me. It was the first hard evidence I go blind in up close encounters, when the early 2000s roommates, co-worker union struggles, dentists office problems and so forth in the passing nudity of on the spot visuals were too strange in mood to what I was normally doing when they happened to me that I couldn't capture the people to take hold of in immediate memory or be real friendly to me– if I can do that in their kindness, for relationship to marry,  perhaps gather testimony and find a good lawyer we will know what happens more to add to all my 4 so far  books partly when not on IP but on conscientious objectors to war on religious grounds, and priest abuses to Protestant children who talk up a storm even if appearing quiet.  That is if I can find law not paid by the Microsoft conflict of interests to represent me unique of a different stripe, creed, or religion. [see chapter 5 Truth to Origin constitution amendment for lover ability as guide to those helping us including professionals]  I ask for treatment worth MHSA CA - '04 Founder of Prop 63 Tax code genesis, a girl friend and wife, and MONEY, awards including with PEACE to USA foe Gregg K. Jann working on.

You may see that however rough and long the fire damage was to California October 2017 I have a long history of not getting credit when I was due- a major point of Truth to Origin.  WE can solve it even if war size, this Piracy issue, with health and no chemical punishments in treatments for human rights, dignity; credit to Gregg K. Jann for source perspective designer of "larking" big things with the small, and pay moulah meaning money which is to Gregg K. Jann in recognition of his "larking" starts and parts of enterprises and projects.  I see non-fiction  as a wise way of getting credit or only way I can afford it for time being and it's a transparency issue for government reform, wondering if lawyers rarely pay maybe don't in a winning lawsuit. I see it like the Union negotiation I won for line staff represented by a labor lawyer and a coordinator position lawyer for my Sacramento ballot initiative design. I hope I can reach out in diplomacy when full credit and money reaches me, with State and Federal Constitution amendment proposal worked up the best known as can be, better with a wife if she were to afford to come on to me.

I guess it, the source perspective designer stolen IP since childhood in many practical fields and professionally applied, boils down to my bragging rights in NE and my father, particularly when he moved to Manhattan, when I was a youth. Low and behold, I survived a subway runaway thinking brave like a DOD defense nut having fun. Such attention-getting sparked a glow which was matter of fact newsworthy, and could have urged inhuman targeting Protestant Gregg when he was studying computer MIS or making speeches to himself. Used royally by "you don't need anything" type of church-thinking of his Reverend father by employed Ordination, and us "You" is rated to be guilty of mental health Catholics who all raped the too decent man away from having family, money, and health prior the CA fire strikes. Does reader see a connection to being in immoral geographic zones aka Sodom and Gomorrah of October 2017 to Catholic priest abuse and abuse of the mental health system and IP theft by Western Capitalism? What's up with Gregg and his family, when he says his A Jann Plan is the most valuable content of any book in history and he lives Working Disabled poverty? Answer Course: Care about beginnings, and how small people they are and bolster kindly. Repair damage to person, even if you were running him for Pope in the Vatican, and/or if he was running for US President, which you can see by my achievements and saintly demeanor although discriminated from easy access to a wife author always wanted and waited for his worth "Eyoiu".

WE CAN WIN THIS THING ABOUT PIRACY, passing into law, talking among the adults, and practices taught in schools to spread over time to all of us from our students: a Peace Initiative for western not just America ideology to un-Pirate the world in a more interactive people oriented economy and stop the stealing of too much from someone. Diversity and dignity to use caution for weakness in persons to build these to their potential, to repair harm to those disabled, and end using poison to take social position and to not nationalize their property, and generally have added care toward fellow man.

Signed: "The Man, The Myth, and The Legend"
who is Gregg K. Jann

www.ingramcontent.com/pod-product-compliance
Lightning Source LLC
Chambersburg PA
CBHW070540290526
45790CB00002B/581